A Women's Mental Health Agenda

A joint project of the
American Psychological Association
Women and Health Roundtable
and
Federation of Organizations for Professional Women

Supported by a grant
from the
Ittleson Foundation

Nancy Felipe Russo, Ph.D., Editor
Arizona State University

Published by the American Psychological Association
1200 Seventeenth Street, N.W.
Washington, DC 20036
September 1985

ISBN: 0-912704-44-6

LC Catalog Card No. 85-72729

Printed in the United States of America

TABLE OF CONTENTS

ACKNOWLEDGEMENTS

This project to develop "A National Agenda to Address Women's Mental Health Needs" was made possible by a grant from the Ittleson Foundation. On behalf of the conference participants and the Advisory Committee, I would like to express our deep appreciation to the Foundation for its support.

The conference, its report, and follow-up activities reflect the work of many people. The Women and Health Roundtable, the Federation of Organizations for Professional Women, and the American Psychological Association all provided substantial support for the project, from its early stages through its completion. The members of the Advisory Committee, who served without reimbursement, spent considerable time reviewing plans for the conference, identifying participants, and developing background materials that have been incorporated into the final report. Carol Burroughs ably served as Conference Coordinator, and Project Associate Susan Seidler helped to develop the conference report and to organize the briefing for its release.

Lorraine Pecarsky and Nina Feldman of the Public Affairs Office of the American Psychological Association organized a press briefing on women's mental health issues in conjunction with the conference. The briefing was well received and resulted in considerable media attention to the conference issues.

Representatives Mary Rose Oakar and Patricia Schroeder deserve special thanks for their sponsorship of the conference breakfast briefing on Capitol Hill, which provided the occasion for the release of the conference report and for the beginning of the process of amplifying and implementing the conference agenda.

Thanks also go to Carolyn Gammon, Cheryl Roberts, Leni Ward, and Jane Winston, for their assistance in preparation of the manuscript.

Although I served as editor for the conference report, it should be considered to have multiple authorship. Material for substantial portions of this report was developed by Ellen Bassuk, M.D.; Carol Burroughs, M.A.; Elaine Carmen, M.D.; Florence Denmark, Ph.D.; Chai Feldblum; Nina Feldman, Ph.D.; Jean Hamilton, M.D.; Mary Jansen, Ph.D.; Linda Silverman King, M.S.W.; Susan Seidler; Diana Zuckerman, Ph.D.; the Women's Task Force of the Michigan Department of Mental Health, and the participants of the working groups. Thanks also go to D. Allen Meyer for commenting on the draft report, and to Deanna Cook of APA's Communications Office for copyediting the manuscript.

Nancy Felipe Russo, Ph.D.
Project Director
January, 1985

EXECUTIVE SUMMARY

EXECUTIVE SUMMARY

On November 16, 1984, fifty leaders representing mental health professions in psychology, psychiatry, social work, medical sociology, and nursing met with advocates and policymakers at an invitational conference to begin to develop a national agenda to address women's mental health needs. This historic conference, which was cosponsored by the American Psychological Association and the Women and Health Roundtable and made possible by a grant from the Ittleson Foundation, had three goals:

1. to assess the status of women's mental health needs;

2. to identify priority areas for attention; and

3. to create an interdisciplinary network to facilitate implementation of the conference recommendations.

The conference addressed issues of access as well as appropriateness of mental health programs and services to women. Research, education and training, and prevention programs were seen as tools for change. However, increasing the participation of women at all levels in the mental health delivery system--as providers and as policymakers--was seen as the first step toward using these tools. That participation was considered a necessary condition for eliminating sex bias and sex role stereotyping in the delivery of mental health services.

The conference participants pointed out that developing appropriate diagnosis, treatment, rehabilitation, and prevention strategies requires recognition of the impact of the social context on women's mental health, a position that challenges traditional intrapsychic, biomedical approaches to mental disorder. The working sessions considered the social, economic, and psychological factors affecting women's mental health and made recommendations for changes needed to create a mental health delivery system able to respond appropriately and positively to the needs of women.

The one-day conference was conceived as the beginning of a process of developing and pursuing a national agenda, not as producing a final concrete outcome. The goals of the conference participants were to establish communication across disciplines, to reach a consensus about the need for united action, and to create a mechanism for achieving that united action over the long term. The reports of the working sessions identify numerous issues in need of dialogue, discussion, and action on federal, state, and local levels.

The recommendations of the working groups span the areas of mental health education, training, service, and research, as well as prevention. These deliberations are a foundation for the development of mental health policies and programs responsive to the needs of both sexes.

The working groups considered and reported on six areas:

I.   Gender and sex bias in mental health education and training, theories and research, and practice.

II.   Women in the family, at work, and in the community.

III.   Diagnosis and treatment--issues of access to and appropriateness of treatment, including psychotropic drugs.

IV.   Physical, sexual, and psychological abuse.

V.   Chronically mentally ill women, homeless women, and inpatient women.

VI.   Special populations: female children and adolescents, midlife women, elderly women, minority women, lesbians, women veterans, and military wives.

Out of the discussions of the working groups a five-part agenda for addressing women's mental health needs emerged:

I.   Increasing the visibility and participation of women in mental health leadership positions.

II.   Increasing the knowledge base about women's mental health, and ensuring that sex bias in research does not detract from the quality of that knowledge base.

III.   Integrating the new research on women, particularly with regard to diagnosis and treatment, into mental health education, training, and practice.

IV.   Examining and improving the impact of current and proposed policies and programs, including financing, on women's mental health research, education, training, and service delivery.

V.   Developing prevention efforts that will address the conflicts and dilemmas experienced by women in their families, work settings, and communities.

The conference participants concluded that organized advocacy across disciplines was needed to bring women's mental health issues to the attention of policymakers and mental health professionals. That advocacy requires a multilevel approach involving outreach to federal and state governments as well as to the private sector.

To implement the conference agenda and to begin organized advocacy, the conference participants voted to establish a National Coalition for Women's Mental Health, charging the Coalition with the tasks of consolidating the communication that had already been established and with beginning a dialogue with policymakers.

INTRODUCTION

INTRODUCTION

The Public Health Service Task Force on Women's Health

The Public Health Service (PHS) Task Force on Women's Health was established in June of 1983 to develop a report on the status of women's health in the United States. During the course of its work, that Task Force became a national focal point for women's issues and for information on women's health, including mental health. In September of 1984, the Task Force forwarded its report, which included recommendations for actions to be taken by federal, state, and local governments; the private sector and voluntary organizations, and individual women themselves, to the Assistant Secretary for Health. That report should serve as the foundation for public policy efforts on behalf of women's health for the coming decade.

The PHS Task Force pointed out that gender plays an important role in the etiology, effects, and treatment of alcohol, drug abuse, and mental illness, but that the nature and extent of that role is poorly understood. In recent years, research has begun to document the complex ways that sex bias, sex role stereotyping, and devaluation of women have affected the nature, diagnosis, and treatment of mental health problems, but the knowledge base is still less than adequate (Russo, 1984a).

Strong, interdisciplinary advocacy is needed if the development of federal and state policies and programs addressing women's mental health is to be a priority.

With the completion of the PHS report, the Task Force as an entity ceased to exist. Currently there is no mechanism at the national level for maintaining the momentum generated by the work of the Task Force. The need for a mechanism to maintain momentum with regard to women's mental health issues is particularly critical. Mental health issues have received only minor attention by advocacy groups devoted to women's health (Lear, 1983). Despite the attention paid to women's mental health issues within the mental health professions (Russo, 1984a), there has been little communication across disciplines.

Strong, interdisciplinary advocacy is needed if the development of federal and state policies and programs addressing women's mental health is to be a priority. Recognition of the need for an interdisciplinary mechanism to maintain policy momentum and to promote understanding of the relationship of gender and sex roles to mental health led to a proposal to the Ittleson Foundation for an interdisciplinary conference on "Developing a National Agenda to Address Women's Mental Health Needs."

The National Coalition for Women's Mental Health

The PHS Task Force pointed out that the nation's leaders must create a climate of concern, as well as new legislative proposals and regulatory changes, in order to give appropriate attention to women's health issues. Since that effort can best succeed if there is substantial community interest, the Task Force recommended that all organizations interested in women's health become better informed regarding legislative, policy, and service issues affecting women's health; promote information exchange on health matters; and advocate organizational and public policy changes to improve and promote women's health. In that context, perhaps the most significant outcome of the conference is the formation of the National Coalition for Women's Mental Health, the first interdisciplinary group specifically devoted to education, research, and advocacy on behalf of women's mental health issues.

Changes in women's work and family roles have occurred despite persistent patterns of sex role stereotyping and sex discrimination. Thus, there are now talented and creative women scientists, administrators, and mental health professionals who have the potential to make a considerable impact on mental health training, research, treatment, and policy development if the barriers to their full and active participation are removed. The National Coalition for Women's Mental Health will provide a voice for these individuals. For information about the Coalition contact NCWMH, Women's Studies Program, Arizona State University, Tempe, AZ 85287.

The Report

The remainder of this report consists of six sections. The first section provides an overview of the status of women's mental health, which provides the background for the conference agenda. The second section presents the five-part agenda, with background information that can be used for advocacy efforts. The third section contains reports from the working groups. Sections IV, V, and VI contain lists of references, advisory committee members, and conference participants, respectively.

To illustrate the extensive networks represented by the persons involved in the project, brief biographies of members of the Advisory Committee are provided. The information contained in these pages should provide a tool for the networking and advocacy at federal, state, and local levels that are needed to effect needed changes in the status of women's mental health.

Section I

The Status of
Women's Mental Health

SECTION I.
THE STATUS OF WOMEN'S MENTAL HEALTH

Over the last decade, significant changes have taken place in our beliefs and expectations about women's roles and identities in the contexts of work, family, and community. These changes have been accompanied by an unprecedented expansion of knowledge and literature, which signifies the attempt to understand and convey the female experience. This new scholarship has identified sex bias in psychological theories and methods, has documented the pervasive and destructive effects of gender inequality, and has examined the stresses that differentially affect women by virtue of their unequal social status, especially in their family roles. Every basic formulation about women's psychology has been questioned and, in many instances, reconceptualized (Carmen, Russo, & Miller, 1981; Rieker & Carmen, 1984; Walker, 1984).

This research tells us that circumstances and conditions that society accepts as normal or ordinary often lead to mental health problems in women. Women face dilemmas and conflicts in the contexts of marriage, family relationships, reproduction, childrearing, divorce, aging, education, and work. Incest, rape, and marital violence also increase risk of mental disorder.

Epidemiological data link mental disorder with alienation, powerlessness, and poverty, conditions that hallmark women's disadvantaged economic status. The specific forms of psychological distress suffered by women seem closely related to the convergence of these factors (Carmen, et al., 1981). The existence of this new knowledge challenges mental health professionals to explore how the social context contributes to the origin and persistence of the problems of their clients and to develop programs of prevention.

Rates and Patterns of Mental Disorder for Women

The large and complex differences in rates and patterns of mental disorder reveal that understanding the relationship of gender, sex roles, and mental health is necessary for the development of cost-effective mental health policies and programs.

Psychological distress occurs more frequently among women than among men.

Women report more worries and say more often than do men that they have felt they were going to have a nervous breakdown. Women say more frequently that bad things happen to them more often and feel overwhelmed by bad events that happen. They experience more feelings of inadequacy as parents, report slightly more psychological anxiety, and endorse slightly lower self-evaluation and personal efficacy statements than do men (Veroff, Kulka, & Douvan, 1981).

**Frequencies and patterns of mental disorder are vastly different
for women and men.**

Patterns of mental disorder differ markedly in women and men for both
noninstitutionalized and institutionalized populations. The most recent survey
data available, from the widely acclaimed NIMH Epidemiological Catchment
Area Program, shows that in 1980 for the noninstitutionalized population:

● Women showed substantially higher rates of depressive disorders and
phobias by a factor of at least two to one. In contrast, men showed higher
rates of antisocial personality and alcohol abuse/dependence.

● Women were more likely to be diagnosed as having dysthymic
disorders, somatization disorders, panic disorders, obsessive/compulsive
disorders, and schizophrenia.

● For both sexes, the highest rates for most mental disorders were found
in the 25 to 44 age range, but this finding is particularly true for women.
Compared to men, women have higher prevalence rates of affective disorders
at every age.

● Although men have higher rates of substance abuse (alcohol and drug
abuse), the gender difference in drug abuse/dependence is smaller at younger
ages, implying that the pattern of differences may change in future
generations (Regier et al., 1984).

**Women are more likely than are men to use mental health services,
particularly outpatient services, but men are more likely to be seen
by mental health professionals.**

In 1977, an estimated 5.6 percent of females of all ages compared with
3.5 percent of males of all ages visited ambulatory health care services (in
either the specialty mental health care or general medical health care sectors)
for treatment of a mental health-related problem (Horgan, 1982).

Of persons identified as having one of the disorders described in the NIMH
Catchment Area Survey, although a higher proportion of women than men
made mental health visits, men were more likely to be seen by a mental health
specialist than by a general service provider. In contrast, nearly one-half of
women's mental health visits were made in the general medical sector,
suggesting that primary physicians play a disproportionate role in the
treatment of women's mental health problems as compared to men's.

There are dramatic differences in utilization patterns by age, sex, and race/ethnicity across type of facility.

A higher percentage of women than men receive services from various types of facilities. For example, in 1975, of people receiving services from private mental health facilities, 57 percent were women; from general hospital inpatient units, 63 percent were women; from outpatient psychiatric facilities 55 percent were women. The situation reversed in state and county mental hospitals and in public mental hospitals. The extent of the difference varied with race/ethnicity. Women were less than one percent of all patients in Veterans Administration hospitals (Russo & Sobel, 1981).

The conflicts and dilemmas associated with work and family roles are associated with higher rates of mental disorder for both sexes.

For both sexes, married individuals utilize mental health facilities at lower rates than do single, widowed, or divorced individuals. The importance of examining the relationship of work and family roles and mental health for women is seen in the findings that:

● Low income mothers in single headed households with young children have been found to have the highest depression rate of any demographic group.

● The number of female heads of single parent households that utilizes mental health facilities exceeds the number of married women by more than four to one.

● Marital difficulty is the most commonly reported event in the six months prior to the onset of depression and the most frequent problem presented and discussed by depressed women in outpatient treatment.

● Divorce is associated with a substantial change in financial status. The income of divorced mothers typically drops to one-half to even one-third of the level before the divorce, whereas expenses remain essentially the same since women are typically given custody of their children.

● For displaced homemakers the stress of divorce is compounded by the stress of reentry into the job market for women who are untrained and unfamiliar with job routines and pressures. There are an estimated 150,000 displaced homemakers, 110,000 of which fall below the poverty line.

● One out of five women experience the stress of widowhood by age 65; and two out of three by age 74 (Women's Task Force, 1983).

Disproportionate rates of psychological disorder among women reflect the higher expected rates of disorder among married women, particularly among married minority women.

Men have higher rates of admission to mental health facilities than do women for all marital status categories, with one exception--married men have lower admission rates than do married women. This reversal is especially dramatic for minority women (Russo & Sobel, 1981).

Since married persons have lower rates of mental illness than do persons in other marital status categories, it has been suggested that marriage confers mental health benefits (Gove, Hughes, & Style, 1983). The extent of the alleged benefits differs, however, depending on both gender and race. Developing an index based on the proportional differences between the rates of the married and the never married, we find that marriage is associated with a 71 percent reduction in illness rates for minority men, 63 percent for white men, 28 percent for white women, and 8 percent for minority women (Carmen, et al., 1981).

Despite clear and substantial differences in rates and patterns of mental disorder and of utilization of mental health services, such differences have yet to be appropriately researched; the factors underlying them are not understood.

Inappropriate conclusions about gender differences in mental health and disorder continue to be drawn from studies that are not adequately designed for testing those differences. These conclusions are presented to the public in misleading ways, ways that are potentially harmful because they detract attention from the substantial gender differences in rates and patterns of disorder that exist. A recent, widely publicized example is found in the interpreting and reporting of the preliminary NIMH Catchment Area Survey results.

Although the Catchment Area Program has been heralded as a landmark in psychiatric epidemiology and research, only 15 disorders are covered in the initial survey instrument. Thus, statements about overall rate of psychiatric disorder from the initial wave of this research are inappropriate.

Nonetheless, misleading statements were released to the press to the effect that the study's failure to find gender differences in the total overall rates of the disorders covered was a new and significant contribution, and in contradiction to earlier work. In fact, the findings did not contradict the thrust of earlier work, and the overall rate reported reflects the rates only of the particular disorders chosen for inclusion in the study.

The inability of the survey to describe overall rates and patterns of mental disorder is evidenced in its finding that one-third of the persons identified as making mental health visits were not identified as having one of the fifteen disorders covered by the survey instrument. Among the disorders omitted from the survey at this stage were generalized anxiety disorder and post-traumatic stress disorder, two diagnoses particularly important for victims of physical and sexual violence.

Selected Areas of Concern

The conference agenda can be applied to a variety of content areas. Selected areas are presented here as background information in order to communicate the range, severity, complexity, and interrelatedness of women's mental health problems. All of them reveal the need for a more adequate knowledge base, trained service providers, and policies and programs that attend to the special concerns of women. This information makes clear that a thorough understanding of gender, sex roles, and mental health is critical if we are to train competent personnel and design effective mental health services.

Depression

Depression is the leading diagnosis for both white and black women. There is substantial documentation that more women than men are depressed in a ratio of about two to one. Gender differences in utilization rates are most prominent in outpatient services where female rates are triple those for males in the 25 to 44 age group (Belle, 1980). Evidence for the preponderence of depression in women comes from clinical sources as well as from population surveys of people not in treatment. Klerman and Weissman (1980) estimate that 20 to 30 percent of all women experience depressive episodes at some point during their lives, often of moderate severity. In contrast to past stereotypes that link menopause and depression, it appears that young poor women who head single-parent families and young married women who work at dead-end jobs have shown the greatest rise in the rate of both treated and untreated depression (Belle, 1980; Guttentag, Salasin, & Belle, 1980).

When the victim of physical abuse accepts a sedative as a means of surviving the brutality, when the homemaker believes she can salvage a marital relationship by drinking, we must rethink our priorities and services.

The thoughtful work of Belle and her colleagues serves to underscore the role of powerlessness in the development of psychological distress (Belle, 1982). Women who became depressed had previously made many varied attempts to cope. Those with the highest rate of depression, that is, the low-income mothers, were continuously faced with multiple and chronic stresses affecting both their children and themselves. Efforts to deal with these conditions led to repeated frustration over employment possibilities, housing conditions, protection against violence and crime, child-care assistance, and the insensitive attitudes and responses of social service and mental health agencies. As Guttentag and Salasin (1976) conclude, "stress and powerlessness apparently are the deadly combination."

Biological, endocrinologic, and genetic factors, as presently understood, are not sufficient to explain gender differences in depression. There are, however, a wide variety of stresses that directly or indirectly have more impact on women and contribute to higher risk for this disorder: physical and sexual abuse, sexual harassment, sex discrimination, childbearing and childrearing, unwanted pregnancy, divorce, poverty, and powerlessness (Carmen, Russo, & Miller, 1981).

We need to increase our knowledge base about psychological factors contributing to depression, particularly in ethnic minority and older women. Further, service providers must learn about the range of factors that underlie depression and develop treatment plans that take into account that range of factors. Reliance on drugs as the preferred treatment for depression overlooks the contribution of social and cognitive factors to the origin and persistence of women's symptoms.

The Subpanel on the Mental Health of Women, in a report to the President's Commission on Mental Heath (1978) expressed this concern as follows: "When the victim of physical abuse accepts a sedative as a means of surviving the brutality, when the homemaker believes she can salvage a marital relationship by drinking, we must rethink our priorities and services."

Physical and Sexual Abuse

As Lois Haight Herrington (1985) has reported, "During the course of the President's Task Force on Victims of Crime, one kind of victim was found nearly everywhere and yet was uniquely abandoned--the victim of family violence" (p. 100). Physical and sexual abuse, particularly in the family, has profound implications for the mental health of both sexes, but particularly for women, who are most likely to experience violence.

As Dobash and Dobash have pointed out (1979), "It is within marriage that a woman is most likely to be slapped and shoved about, severely assaulted, killed, or raped." Nearly one in five of murder victims in 1983 were killed by a family member; of female homicide victims, nearly one-third were killed by husbands or boyfriends. Family violence is a widespread, pervasive social problem, extending across all socioeconomic, cultural, religious, and educational categories. It happens at all ages, from infancy to old age.(Herrington, 1985).

A serious social consequence of physical and sexual abuse is that it is transmitted from generation to generation. Children who are abused or witness abuse in their families are more likely as adults to become either victims or perpetrators of family violence. Researchers estimate that one out of three male offenders has been a victim of sexual abuse and that victims of abuse have a greater likelihood of becoming sexual offenders (Center for Women's Policy Studies, 1984).

A recent study of an inpatient population has gone beyond the link between child abuse and criminality, establishing a relationship been abuse and severe psychiatric disorder (Carmen, Rieker, & Mills, 1984). In that study

• 53 percent of all female and 23 percent of all male patients had abuse histories;

• 89 percent of the sexually abused patients were female.

This research provides further confirmation that female adults and children of both sexes are at highest risk for violence within the family. In addition, it contrasts the alarming numbers of people who are physically and sexually abused and the relative lack of attention given these topics in taking routine psychiatric histories.

Mythical but widely held clinical beliefs [about battered women] result in misdiagnosis, inappropriate treatment, and failure to protect the victim.

Battered women exhibit a wide range of emotional and behavioral symptoms as a result of repeated abuse. Practitioners often misinterpret these disturbances as a sign of mental illness in the victim rather than as a response to ongoing physical and psychological danger. Psychological theories that blame the victim and protect the assailant--for example, the view that the battered wife needs and provokes the abuse for masochistic reasons--contribute to the problems of battered women. These mythical but widely held clinical beliefs result in misdiagnosis, inappropriate treatment, and failure to protect the victim (Women's Task Force, 1983).

Sex-role expectations contribute to spouse abuse. It is in rigidly traditional families that female adults and children are at highest risk for violence and sexual abuse.

As the PHS Task Force pointed out, too little research has been directed toward understanding the roots of violence against women. Evidence suggests, however, that sex-role expectations and social and cultural attitudes that accept violence as a way to assert power and control are major factors contributing to spouse abuse. It is in rigidly traditional families that female adults and children are at highest risk for violence and sexual abuse (Carmen, Russo, & Miller, 1981; Hilberman, 1980).

Such abuse may even be supported in the name of religion. Castelli (1984) has pointed out that some fundamentalist parents believing in "spare the rod and spoil the child" have applied "discipline" that has resulted in severe injury or death. Similarly, in the name of fundamentalist Christian religion, state and federal child abuse laws and support for shelters for battered women have been attacked. Involving religious leaders in programs to prevent physical and sexual abuse may be an important strategy for prevention.

We need to learn more about the short- and long-term consequences of sexual abuse in childhood. Consider the following findings (Department of the Navy, 1983; King, 1981):

● Retrospective studies suggest a very high incidence of sexual abuse of children. In the majority of these cases, the offender is known to the victim.

● One-fifth to one-third of adult females report a childhood sexual experience with an adult male, according to large surveys of mostly white, middle-class women.

● Incest is estimated to occur in 14 percent of families and is found in all family types and social classes.

● In three out of four reported cases, incest occurs between fathers and daughters. Current research suggests that when boys are sexually abused within their families, they are also likely to be victimized by adult males.

● Even infants have been physically and sexually abused. However, the peak years of abuse occur in children of between eight and twelve years of age.

● Incest is usually not a single, isolated incident, but an extended process lasting over a period of years.

● Incest usually continues until intervention occurs, but children are often confused and do not know where to turn for help.

● Physically abusive parents tend to be isolated from social networks. In comparing abusive and nonabusive mothers, abusive mothers were found to have fewer contacts with family, neighbors, or friends and infrequently engaged in social or recreational activities.

Prevention of physical and sexual abuse of women is an essential element of any national program aimed at promoting mental health and preventing mental illness.

These findings suggest that effective intervention cases requires the cooperation of community organizations including police, the courts, social services, hospitals, and mental health agencies to ensure protection for victims. Furthermore, prevention of physical and sexual abuse of women is an essential element of any national program aimed at promoting mental health and preventing mental illness.

Chronically Mentally Ill Women

The chronically mentally ill have been recognized nationally as a high priority treatment group. However, gender differences have barely been considered. There is a tendency to consider such women as genderless persons (Test & Berlin, 1981) and treatment is male-oriented. Yet, to the extent that differences have been identified through experience, anecdote, or case studies, the results suggest that chronically mentally ill women have different and more extensive problems than men while treatment is male-oriented.

The conference participants pointed out that in discussing the needs of chronically mentally ill women, assessing the status of subpopulations is necessary. These are:

• The aging with mental disorders,

• Young chronically mentally ill women,

• Midlife women, particularly with regard to chronic problems of mentally ill with marginal skills,

• Homeless single females,

• Homeless women with children,

• Chronically mentally ill women in community programs,

• Institutionalized women,

• Women with dual diagnosis of mental illness and substance abuse,

• Women with dual diagnosis of mental illness and developmental disabilities.

Chronically mentally ill women are more likely to be sexually active than are chronically mentally ill men. Although a substantial number of these women have children, little is known about them as mothers. Their relative lack of birth control information and contraception combined with vulnerability to rape and exploitive sexual relationships suggest that the frequency of unwanted pregnancies among chronically mentally ill women may be substantial. In one study, 54 percent of female inpatients (compared to 38 percent of the men) reported having sexual intercourse the previous month (Women's Task Force, 1983).

Sex education and information on birth control is critical to this group of women who often find themselves vulnerable to sexual victimization. Contributing factors include insecure housing, unsafe neighborhoods, and lack of experience and role models for appropriate sexual behavior. There are many instances in which chronically mentally ill women have given consent to have sexual relationships with men either without fully understanding their own bodies or because they lack assertiveness.

Policies that address issues of chronically mentally ill women must also take into account that:

● Treatment approaches and interventions for the long-term mentally disabled who are mothers are almost nonexistent. The stress of mentally disabled mothers is compounded by the fact that their children are also at higher risk for emotional disturbance and by professionals who blame mothers for their children's problems.

● Women generally have more chronic health problems than do men. These problems, or the side effects of medications prescribed for them, may cause or exacerbate psychiatric problems.

● Psychotropic medication used to treat chronically mentally ill women may also have side effects that have special implications for women's self-esteem and body image. These drugs affect appearance (e.g., weight gain, acne) and health (e.g., menstrual irregularities, possible relationship with breast cancer, vaginal lubrication), but these side effects are infrequently addressed.

● Clinicians often assume that a return to the family is the best outcome for mentally disabled women, without considering that the family structure itself may have significantly contributed to the women's problems (Women's Task Force, 1983).

Women who are long-term mentally disabled are at a greater economic disadvantage than are men. One study of chronic patients found men's average income to be $220 per month, whereas women's income averaged $36 per month. Referrals to vocational training programs are less frequent for women and when they do occur, training is usually for poorly paid, traditionally female occupations. Rehabilitation programs have been found to reflect the goal of equipping men to become economically productive while reinforcing traditional expectations of "learned helplessness" for women (Russo & Jansen, in press; Smith & Smith, 1980).

As Bachrach (1984) points out in her review of the literature, deinstitutionalization policies have a special impact on chronically mentally ill women, particularly in such areas as exploitation and violence, homelessness, diversion into the criminal justice system, and stigma. Although the provision of services is inadequate for both chronically mentally ill men and women, there is evidence, in some areas of the country at least, that scarcity of shelter space is greater for women. Further, intake policies and regulations for women's shelters are often more restrictive than are those for men's shelters (Baxter & Hopper, 1982).

The population of elderly chronically mentally ill is also of particular concern. Women predominate in that population, accounting for 71 percent of the chronically mentally ill living in nursing homes (Cicchinelli et al., 1981). As Bachrach notes, problems specific to the aged mentally ill, such as inappropriate placement and increased mortality risk associated with transfer, are largely women's problems.

There is also a neglect by policymakers and service providers of the needs of family members, usually mothers, who have the burden of caring for the deinstitutionalized. As Thurer (1983) observes, such mothers already suffer from the pain of coping with illness in their children and from the stigma and guilt of being considered by many, perhaps even including themselves, to be the cause of the problem. These women are asked to oversee a treatment plan, no matter how unrealistic in terms of time, energy, money, and the demands of the rest of the family and to do this with little outside support, conflicting professional advice, and little expectancy of success (Thurer, 1983).

Homeless Women

In the 1980s, the numbers of homeless persons have increased. Estimates of the numbers in 1984 range from 250,000 to 3 million--1 percent of the total population. Unlike previous decades when the majority of homeless persons were unattached, middle-aged, alcoholic men, the population today is becoming progressively younger and includes increasing numbers of individual women and female-headed families. According to a survey by the Department of Health and Human Services (DHHS), it is estimated that 65 percent of the homeless are single men, 15 percent are single women, and 20 to 30 percent are family members (DHHS, 1984a).

Family shelter directors report that the vast majority of homeless families are made up of single mothers and young children, many below the age of five. A number of the women are welfare mothers evicted from their homes. Others may have spouses who have deserted them, are abusive, or are mentally ill and incapable of caring for them. The number of family shelters has proliferated within the last few years in response to the growing need. Although many are open 24 hours a day, they provide only rudimentary services.

One consequence of the physical and sexual abuse in childhood described above is an increasing population of homeless youth--youth between 16 and 21 years of age living apart from their families. According to a recent report by the Homeless Youth Steering Committee (HYSC) of the New York State Council on Children, Youth, and Families, one study concluded that 64 percent of runaway youth had conditions in their family households that were dangerous to their physical or emotional well-being (HYSC, 1984).

In 1978 an estimated 84 percent of homeless youth had been hit by their parents; more than one in two had been beaten at least one a month, and one out of four had been beaten every day. More than two out of three of those who had been hit by their parents reported that a mark or scar had resulted from the violence. Sexual abuse was also found to be a contributing factor to homelessness.

The population of homeless youth is about half male and half female. However the average age of females is significantly lower than that of males (15 vs. 17 years), and these females have special needs. They have a high rate of sexual activity. One study of homeless youth reported that one-third of the females had been pregnant at least once. A recent study in New York City reported that 70 percent of of the homeless youth to showed symptoms of mental disorder, with more than 33 percent of the females and 15 percent of the males having made at least one attempt at suicide. Another study in New York City reported that one in five females had a previous arrest record (HYSC, 1984).

Seventy percent of homeless youth showed symptoms of mental disorder, with more than 33 percent of the females and 15 percent of the males having made at least one attempt at suicide.

The characteristics of the homeless population vary with geography. However, the largest numbers of the homeless--in some areas from 65 to 75 percent--are those who suffer from chronic disabilities--mental illness, alcohol abuse, drug abuse, or combinations of these problems. Estimates of those who are homeless due to recent economic setbacks range from 35 to 40 percent. In addition, it is thought that 10 to 15 percent of the homeless are on the streets or in emergency shelters due to personal crises such as domestic violence, divorce, desertion, or health-related problems (DHHS, 1984b).

Individual homeless women appear to exhibit a higher rate of serious mental illness than men. A study of homeless persons living on skid row in Los Angeles showed that 75 percent of the males and 90 percent of the females were suffering from chronic, incapacitating psychiatric illness (Bassuk, Rubin, & Lauriat, 1984). A Boston shelter estimates that 50 percent of its males and 90 percent of its females are mentally disabled (American Psychiatric Association, 1984). In comparison to the men, the women are more often psychotic and more frequently have a history of psychiatric treatment, including hospitalization.

The causal relationship between homelessness and mental illness goes both ways. Certainly the stress, alienation, and violence experienced by the homeless on the streets increase the risk of mental disorder. In addition, some of the chronically mentally ill are homeless due to the deinstitutionalization of state hospitals and other changes in the mental health system over the past 25 years. Many of these people were released from institutions with no place to go. Most communities did not have facilities or programs for these discharged patients, and many of them ended up on the streets.

There is also a new generation of chronically mentally ill who were not eligible for hospitalization because their disorders developed after changes in the mental health laws. Their numbers have increased, as the large baby boom cohorts have entered the age range of 25 to 45--the years of highest risk for mental disorder.

Systematic research about homeless women, families, and their children is sparse. There is a critical need for controlled studies to establish how their needs and problems are different from men's, particularly among those who are chronically mentally ill. For the present, we must rely on the information at hand—case studies, anecdotal comments, and descriptive reports—which indicate some important areas that need further study.

A study of homeless persons living on skid row in Los Angeles showed that 75 percent of the males and 90 percent of the females were suffering from chronic, incapacitating psychiatric illness (Bassuk et al., 1984).

In contrast to homeless families, homeless individuals are housed in a different shelter network. These facilities provide food, clothes, and a bed, but are generally closed during the day. Therefore, in addition to receiving only rudimentary services, homeless women who are alone are often forced into the streets much of the time. Not having a place to go during the day is more of a problem for elderly persons, pregnant women, and the mentally ill, the groups least able to deal with the rigors of being on the streets (HUD, 1984).

In one study of homeless women (Depp & Ackiss, 1984), the history of their psychiatric treatment indicated that most had only had brief periods of care from the public mental health system. For whatever reasons—apathy, distrust, fear, lack of accessibility, leaving care against medical advice—these women had not used the conventional system. Obviously, it was not working for them. The consequences can be fatal:

> On January 27, 1982, a 61-year-old former psychiatric patient (and college valedictorian) was found dead in her cardboard-box "home" in a New York City street. She had been living in the box for eight months, since her public assistance benefits had been revoked in May of 1981 for "failure to appear for certification." She had rebuffed the efforts of various agencies to relocate her. She died of hypothermia just hours before a court order directing her removal to a hospital for evaluation was secured. (American Psychiatric Association, 1984)

Most homeless women have few, if any, marketable skills with which to support their families. The children have serious difficulties as well. They are frequently the victims of abuse and suffer from various developmental problems. Their problems are compounded by the fact that even if they did not suffer from abuse at home, these children and their mothers are targets for physical and sexual abuse once they are on the streets.

Life on the streets and in the shelters is hazardous for women. It is the impression of many persons working with homeless women that a vast majority have been assaulted or raped. Even if they are not assaulted, women who share shelters with men are often neglected.

Within most shelters women are often targets for abuse.

The subgroup of homeless women for whom the shelters may be the most inadequate are those who are chronically mentally ill. According to one mental health professional, "Shelters are turning into mini-institutions lacking the services available at the old mental hospitals--no one wants responsibility for the chronically mentally ill" (Bassuk et al., 1984). Although more than three-quarters of all shelters provide psychological counseling or referrals, much of it is informal and provided by counselors who are not professionally trained.

There is also a new generation of chronically mentally ill who were not eligible for hospitalization because their disorders developed after changes in the mental health laws. Their numbers have increased, as the large baby boom cohorts have entered the age range of 25 to 45--the years of highest risk for mental disorder.

A number of studies indicate that a majority of the homeless have had little or no contact with family or friends (Levine, 1984). Similar to most homeless persons, homeless women are profoundly disconnected from social supports with one significant exception: A surprisingly high number of them still maintain contact with their children. This finding suggests that if there were a system providing sufficient training and financial, social, and mental health services support, many of the families of these women might be able to assume partial or full responsibility for their care. However, many of these women will not be willing or able to return to their families and will need a range of housing options including emergency shelters, transitional living facilities, and permanent shelter, as well as a broad array of community-based services (Levine, 1984).

Women and Drugs

Although women have severe problems with drug abuse, only recently have these problems been addressed by researchers and policymakers. Our knowledge base is inadequate, and drug treatment programs continue to be oriented toward male users of illegal drugs such as heroin.

As the National Institute of Drug Abuse (1983) has pointed out, in 1980, over half of the patients treated in hospital emergency rooms for drug-related episodes were women. That year, 28 percent of the clients admitted to federally-funded drug treatment facilities were women. These women represented significant proportions of clients in certain drug categories:

- 51 percent of all persons treated for tranquilizer abuse;

- 38 percent of those treated for abuse of other sedatives;

- 35 percent of clients treated for amphetamine abuse;

- 34 percent of persons treated for barbituate abuse; and

- 33 percent of those treated for abuse of opiates other than heroin.

The NIDA report thoroughly reviews the relevant literature, including the history and current status of research on women and drugs. It points out the severity of the problem of women's drug abuse. For example, the regular use of multiple psychoactive drugs in combination with regular consumption of alcohol is widespread among women of childbearing age:

- Between 750,000 and 1,000,000 women of childbearing age are regular, high-frequency users of alcohol plus psychoactive drugs;

- 585,000 are current or regular users of barbituates, with probably no more than three-quarters taking these drugs as prescribed;

- 675,000 are current or regular users of prescription stimulants and appetite depressants, with less than half taking these drugs as prescribed;

- 125,000 use prescription narcotics, and about 100,000 use prescription antidepressants.

The discussion of the problems of older women later in this report reveals that the problems of drug use are not limited to women of childbearing age.

As the NIDA report observed, "...many of the problems of female drug abusers are neither less than, the same, nor more than those of male abusers, but are, instead, unique to the female abuser and in need of their own point of reference" (NIDA, 1983, p. 1). NIDA also points out that race must be considered in developing any conceptual framework for understanding drug abuse--there are substantial race differences in how addicts become addicted, what drugs they use, and how drugs are obtained and administered.

Treatment programs for female addicts are not equipped to attract or retain women in need of services, and they do not respond to the emotional or vocational needs of women clients. Women who drop out of treatment programs have a particularly high rate of psychological disturbance, negative familial circumstances, severe forms of alcohol and drug abuse, and depression (Cuskey, Berger, & Densen-Garber, 1977), suggesting that mental health services could play a critical role in drug treatment programs.

Prescription Drugs More than two-thirds of all prescriptions for psychotropic drugs written in this country each year are for women (Fidell, 1981). Although women make 58 percent of all visits to physicians' offices, they receive 73 percent of all prescriptions written for psychotropic medication (and 90 percent when the prescribing physician is not a psychiatrist). Even psychiatrists, who are trained in the diagnosis and treatment of mental disorder, show evidence of sex bias in prescribing. A national sample of office-based physicians (Cypress, 1980) found that male psychiatrists prescribed drugs about twice as often per office visit as did female psychiatrists, and male psychiatrists tended to prescribe drugs to a higher percentage of women patients (37 percent) than to men patients (28 percent).

Although women make 58 percent of all visits to physicians' offices, they receive 73 percent of all prescriptions written for psychotropic medication (and 90 percent when the prescribing physician is not a psychiatrist).

There is little or no evidence for greater drug-seeking behavior among women when patterns of illicit drug use are examined, however. How then do we understand the sex difference in psychotropic drug use when the source of drugs is a physician? A simple hypothesis is that the gender difference merely parallels the known gender differences in the rates of psychiatric symptoms and syndromes. One survey found that physicians felt that women display more mental disorders, social problems, and other "vague" symptoms than do men and that physicians in general expect women to be less stoic than men during illness.

However, a careful examination of the prescription rates argues against this belief. For example, over the past five years, women are estimated to have received from 71 percent to 83 percent of the prescriptions for antidepressants (Cottler & Robins, 1983; Hughes & Brewin, 1979). The latter figure well exceeds the 66 percent that would be expected based on the epidemiological finding of a two-to-one female-to-male ratio for depressive symptoms and syndromes.

We need to increase our knowledge base about the dynamics of the prescribing process and how sex bias and sex role stereotyping affect it. For example, there may be a greater likelihood of physicians' perceiving a woman's illness as psychosomatic (cf., Armitage, Schneiderman, & Bass, 1979; Lennane & Lennane, 1981; Wallen, Waitzkin, & Stoekle, 1979). A focus on women in drug advertising (Moore, 1980) may both express and reinforce this stereotypic notion.

Sex Bias in Psychotropic Drug Research

Despite the fact that more women than men are given psychotropic drugs, there has been very little concern over the past ten years with the relative adequacy of our data base on women and drugs (Cooperstock, 1978). The data that are available, however, strongly suggest that there are clinically significant gender- and hormone-related effects of psychotropic drugs (Halbreich, Asnis, & Goldstein 1984, Hamilton & Parry, 1983, Lloyd & Alagna, 1984).

Although twice as many women as men are treated for depression, the depression literature suggests that it is the men rather than the women who benefit most from the antidepressant drugs.

In a review of age and gender differences in the response of adults to antidepressants, Raskin (1974) concluded that although "twice as many women as men are treated for depression, the depression literature suggests that it is the men rather than the women who benefit most from the antidepressant drugs" (cf., an update on his review by Hamilton et al., 1984). Women are underrepresented in the early stages of clinical drug testing, partly as a result of FDA Guidelines (Kinney, Trautmann, & Gold, 1981) . The exclusion of young women from early clinical trials directly results in the absence of accurate and complete information about how best to use drugs in women. For many clinical trials, gender and age distributions of the subjects are not readily available (Hamilton et al., 1984).

Many protocols use the same dosage of the drug without reference to weight, despite the fact that women weigh less on the average than men, so that the optimal dosage (to maximize responsivity and to minimize side effects) for each sex remains unassessed. The possible effects of hormonal status on optimal dosages is also understudied. One consequence of our lack of knowledge may be that we inadvertently screen drugs for efficacy in men (e.g., Raskin, 1974) and may discard drugs that might have been more effective in women under certain hormonal conditions.

Kinney and colleagues (1981) point out that the policy of excluding young women from new drug trials only postpones the use of a drug by young women, because women are not subsequently discouraged from taking the drug once it reaches the market. In fact, women may actually take the drug more often than men. It is at this point that more adverse side effects are likely to be discovered.

Hamilton et al. (1984) argue that a comparative gender-related psychopharmacology must be developed to enhance the benefits of drugs--as one treatment strategy among many--in subgroups that are defined by gender, age, and hormonal status.

One study found that 54 percent of women questioned felt that it was better to take drugs than to go through a day tense and nervous, and 48 percent felt it was better to use drugs than to spend a sleepless night.

Pharmacological research also needs to assess the psychological and social consequences of psychotropic drug use in women (Russo, 1984a). For example, one study found that 54 percent of women questioned felt that it was better to take drugs than to go through a day tense and nervous, and 48 percent felt it was better to use drugs than to spend a sleepless night.

Whitman and Duffy (1961) found that newly admitted patients treated exclusively with drugs significantly shifted their beliefs toward viewing their condition as having a physical origin, even to the extent of overlooking the social and interpersonal context in which the dysfunction arose. In a society that devalues women, women all too often begin to devalue themselves (e.g., via the "biology is destiny" notion), and to make self-attributions for their problems. Thus, the preference for drug treatment in women may inadvertently strengthen their tendency toward a kind of learned helplessness (Hamilton, Alagna, & Sharpe, in press).

Alcohol Abuse and Alcoholism in Women

As the PHS Task Force pointed out, alcohol has greater effects on women than men. Yet, because of the stigma of alcohol abuse and alcoholism in women, the needs of alcoholic women have been ignored and misdiagnosis is of major concern. We do know that women begin abusive drinking for different reasons than men. Female alcoholics are older than male alcoholics and are likely to have suffered a recent loss or family crisis that precipitated their drinking. They more readily link drinking to external stress than male alcoholics (National Institute on Alcohol Abuse and Alcoholism [NIAAA], 1983).

Although women who develop problems with alcohol show different patterns and characteristics than do men, most of the major alcohol studies have used male samples. The PHS Task Force pointed out that there are large areas in which the knowledge base with regard to alcohol abuse is inadequate or nonexistent.

The interactive effects of gender and race/ethnicity on alcohol abuse need to be explored, as do marital and family roles:

● Black women, compared to white women, are more likely to be alcohol abstainers by almost a 2 to 1 margin (42 to 25 percent); but of women who do drink, black women are more likely to be heavy drinkers by almost a 2 to 1 margin (11 to 6 percent).

● Rates of alcoholism for black women are higher than for white women. For blacks, the male-female ratio for alcohol problems is 3:2; for whites the ratio is 4:1 to 5:1.

● Female alcoholics frequently marry men who are alcoholics or have a history of psychiatric disorder. These marriages are often unstable, resulting in a high rate of separation and divorce.

● Husbands of alcoholic women are less tolerant of their spouses' drinking than are wives of alcoholic men. Men are more likely to leave alcoholic spouses and fight for custody of children.

● A woman married to an alcoholic husband is often suspected of contributing to the drinking problem, whereas a man married to an alcoholic wife is regarded as deprived and receives sympathy for his burdens (NIAAA, 1983).

Alcoholism is associated with depression--an estimated 35 percent of alcoholics have a current or past history of depressive symptoms. Female alcoholics are more often diagnosed as clinically depressed than are male alcoholics, and they have lower self-esteem. One consequence of the signficant correlation between alcoholism and depression is that many women combine the use of alcohol and psychotropic drugs.

Alcoholic women are more likely than men to use other drugs along with alcohol. An estimated 60 to 70 percent of female alcoholics use sedatives and tranquilizers, primarily Valium. The combination of such drugs and alcohol can be serious and result in death. Yet studies of patterns and incidence of drug abuse in alcoholism are rare.

An estimated 60 to 70 percent of female alcoholics use sedatives and tranquilizers, primarily Valium.

While men appear more likely to abuse alcohol, the consequences of such abuse are more significant for women. Alcoholic women have higher morbidity and mortality rates than men. For example, women develop more extensive liver damage earlier in their drinking history. There is also a significant difference in the rates of suicide attempts in the alcoholic population: Alcoholic women outnumber alcoholic men in both attempted and completed suicides.

Older Women

There are significantly more older women than men in the United States, and their numbers are rapidly increasing. In fact, older women are the fastest growing segment of our population. Despite expanded awareness of and concern for older women, many stereotypes persist that negatively affect the quality of their lives and, thus, their mental health. For older women, the social denigration and devalued status of women is compounded by the denigration and devaluation of the aged generally in U.S. society. If the negative effects of racism are added to those of agism and sexism, the older black woman is in a state of what gerontologists call "triple" or "multiple jeopardy" (Kimmel, 1974).

Popular images that portray older women as inactive, unhealthy, asexual, unattractive, and ineffectual are prevalent. American society places a high value on efficiency, independence, self-sufficiency, physical attractiveness and vitality, sexual capacity, influence, power, and wealth. The older woman as a productive force in this society is seen as having lost her usefulness (White House Mini-Conference on Older Women, 1981).

One assumption is that most of the elderly cannot live independently and that they require costly institutionalized care. Although 86 percent of the elderly, mostly women, have one or more chronic health problems, 95 percent are able to live in the community. Of the 5 percent living in nursing homes and other institutions, three-quarters are women.

Far more older women have chronic illnesses and/or are institutionalized than men, but only because most of the elderly are women. They are no less independent than older men and, in fact, are often more so. Three-quarters of elderly men live with their wives, whereas only 17 percent live alone or with relatives. In contrast, more than half of all women aged 65 or older are widows, and one-third of all women in this age group live alone.

Women are subject to a number of unique stresses, which often begin in midlife and carry over into their older years. Prevention efforts directed toward midlife women may have a substantial impact on the mental health status of future cohorts of elderly. The wife who remains at home may resent giving up a career; working women often feel the need to be more competent on the job than their male counterparts; a woman who has chosen to be a mother and a homemaker may feel useless when her children leave home or experience depression and abandonment after divorce, separation, or death of a spouse (White House Mini-Conference on Older Women, 1981).

Some stresses are abrupt in onset, such as death or illness of a spouse, other relatives, or friends, and loss of job, income, or home. Others are gradual in onset, such as diminishing physical and mental capacities, chronic illness, and difficulty in maintaining productivity in major activities (Davis & Brody, 1979).

As we have mentioned, depression is the single most pressing problem affecting elderly women's mental health. This acute response to the stresses of life is often misdiagnosed and mistaken for untreatable senile dementia. Alzheimer's disease, an organic brain disorder that is currently receiving considerable public attention, is likely to be mistaken for depression in its early stages (Women's Task Force, 1983).

As long as millions of dollars are devoted to the promotion of tranquilizers as the solution to women's depression and anxiety, we shall continue to be drug abusers.

Often, concerned family members cannot discern if the elderly women's mental health problems are due to physiological or emotional factors or both, causing confusion about how to interpret the symptoms. For many elderly women, the solution provided is psychotropic drugs.

Doctors may offer little, if any, information about any side effects of psychotropic drugs and other medication, thereby subjecting many older women taking several different medicines to confusion, depression and other psychiatric, as well as physical, problems (White House Mini-Conference on Older Women, 1981).

To add to the problem, the Food and Drug Administration has not assumed adequate leadership in sensitizing physicians to the special side effects of drugs used by the elderly, nor has it provoked furthered discussion of geriatric dosages. Premarketing clinical tests of drugs also do not examine long-term and multiple drug use by the elderly, particularly by older women (Seidler, 1984).

As was observed in the White House Mini-Conference on Older Women (1981), all of these factors combine to subject older women to high risk for drug abuse: "As long as millions of dollars are devoted to the promotion of tranquilizers as the first and unfailing solution to women's depression and anxiety, we shall continue to be a nation of drug abusers" (White House Mini-Conference on Older Women, 1981).

Women hate to admit alcoholism because of the stigma attached.

Alcohol abuse also presents some unique problems for older women. Because the older woman who is alcoholic receives less understanding and acceptance than does the alcoholic man, she is more likely to be a "hidden" alcoholic and difficult to identify (White House Mini-Conference on Older Women, 1981).

Groups of older women especially vulnerable to alcohol and drug abuse are (1) isolated and depressed women who live alone; (2) women trapped in unhappy marriages; (3) women institutionalized in nursing homes and psychiatric settings; (4) the non-English-speaking, who are culturally isolated, and (5) those lacking the resources to enter treatment programs.

Even if they had the funds, some women would have difficulty entering a treatment program or facility because of their responsibilties for caring for others. Those who approach facilities as potential clients are often rejected by counselors because younger people are assumed to have better recovery potential. If women do enter treatment facilities, they find them generally oriented toward male clients.

Anxiety is another common problem for elderly women, and social and economic conditions are the primary contributing factors. Financial difficulties and poverty are often accompanied by emotional crises.

The nation's 16.4 million elderly women still bear the brunt of poverty and neglect in America.

Although women account for 59 percent of the noninstitutionalized, aged population, they make up 71 percent of the elderly poor. According to a study prepared for the Congressional Caucus for Women's Issues, "The nation's 16.4 million elderly women still bear the brunt of poverty and neglect in America" (Rix, 1984). In addition to creating anxiety, poverty can lead to depression due to feelings of helplessness and renewed dependency needs for many women. Poverty also tends to obscure individual uniqueness, a problem already associated with the elderly in general (Women's Task Force, 1983).

It is estimated that 80 percent of older adults in need of mental health services do not obtain them. Barriers to mental health intervention include a tradition of keeping one's problems to one's self, lack of transportation, and a reluctance on the part of some clinicians to work with this population (Women's Task Force, 1983). Payment mechanisms are also strongly biased toward encouraging institutionalization and provide limited reimbursement for those older patients seeking outpatient treatment (Gatz, Fuentes, & Pearson, n. d.).

Finally, researchers perpetuate stereotypes and cultural myths about women, adding to a poor self-image on the part of older women. Most sociological and mental health research has not addressed the diverse and rapidly changing population of older women. A great deal more research is needed to provide an adequate base of knowledge for the care of this important group (White House Mini-Conference on Older Women, 1981).

Minority Women

Sex bias continues to detract from the quality of mental health services to both sexes. It is, indeed, a step forward for the designers of mental health services to recognize that women's service needs differ from those of men. Nonetheless, it must be remembered that women, as a group, are heterogeneous. The problems of minority women, handicapped women, young women, and aged women differ. Bias due to ethnicity and age compound the difficulties of designing programs to meet the needs of women as individuals. All women, however, are directly or indirectly affected by sex role stereotyping and sex discrimination. Furthermore, the powerlessness, dependency, and poverty often associated with women's roles and with the devaluation of women's status are destructive to mental health.

There is a dearth of research on how differences in sex role stereotypes and sex role expectations might relate to different patterns of etiology, diagnosis, and treatment of mental disorders in minority women.

The profile of rates and patterns of mental disorders previously discussed revealed large sex and race differences in use of mental health facilities (Russo & Olmedo, 1983; Russo & Sobel, 1981). Differences in utilization statistics reflect many factors, including the differential incidence of mental disorders, differential diagnostic practices, and differential treatment of the sexes and members of minority groups in American society. There is a dearth of research on how differences in sex role stereotypes and sex role expectations might relate to different patterns of etiology, diagnosis, and treatment of mental disorders in minority women. Indeed, research on minority mental health in general is needed, particularly research on processes of immigration and acculturation, which may involve greater cultural contrasts for women.

Information on minority issues in education and training programs for mental health professonals is lacking. Because of the lack of specific information on minority women, clinicians often have little other than stereotypes to rely on in practice. One study found that the mental health of minority groups is usually defined by clinicians in terms of adjustment to the majority culture. In fact, this attitude appears to be the leading cause of underutilization of mental health services by minority people in general (Women's Task Force, 1982).

Many researchers, service providers, and policymakers view minority women as a homogeneous population. Yet, women of color themselves are an extremely heterogeneous population. Mental health professionals must be cautious about the tendency to make generalizations based on the experiences of one racial or ethnic group. For example, most of the research on minority women that does exist deals with black women. Findings from this research should not be generalized to all ethnic minority women.

Sex Role Socialization and Mental Health

Beyond addressing the childhood conditions that are conducive to the development of mental disorder, such as physical and sexual abuse, research must also examine the development of the skills, competence, self-confidence, and self-esteem that provide a foundation for good mental health. There is considerable evidence that girls and boys are treated differently by parents, teachers, and other adults. The encouragement and discouragement offered by adults appear to have a great impact on children's feelings of competence.

Early gender and sex role socialization that fails to equip girls with skills and competence and that undermines self-confidence thus lays a foundation for the development of mental health problems in adulthood (Russo, in press). During the grade school years, girls begin to develop self-doubts about their intellectual competency. Although boys' arithmetic and general aptitude scores are comparable to girls' at grades one to three, the boys develop higher expectations for their performance than do girls. These expectations parallel the expectations of the children's parents, who expect boys to get better marks in arithmetic and girls better marks in reading (Entwisle & Baker, 1983).

By fifth and sixth grades, girls show less positive self-concepts than boys. From early elementary school to college, girls consistently rate their intellectual abilities lower than do boys, despite the fact that girls get better grades and higher aptitude test scores. At the same time, boys overestimate their abilities (Crandall, 1967), and consider themselves stronger, more powerful and dominant than girls. As girls become women, they begin to feel less in control of their fate (Maccoby & Jacklin, 1974).

Girls develop belief in their helplessness to control events by grade school. By the fifth grade, girls are more likely than boys to attribute poor performance in achievement situations to lack of ability rather than to luck or effort. They also show decreased persistence or impaired task performance after failure, under the threat of failure, or when they are being evaluated by adults rather than by peers (Dweck, Davidson, Nelson, &Enna, 1978; Dweck & Gilliard, 1975; Nicholls, 1975).

In other words, after failure, boys chalk it up to bad luck or not trying hard enough. Girls, in contrast, lower their estimation of themselves. Increased evaluative pressure enhances the performance of boys, but impairs that of girls (Dweck & Gilliard, 1975). Parents, teachers, and peers, albeit unintentionally, all contribute to the development of these sex differences in self-confidence and performance.

By young adulthood, the research suggests that men and women express similar feelings of self-worth. However, the men have greater self-confidence in their intellectual skills, leadership skills, and other traditionally masculine abilities (Zuckerman, in press).

Traditional sex role expectations have created separate worlds for the sexes, and have interfered with the mutual communication and respect needed for the development of nonexploitive sexual relationships. As we have seen from the discussions above, they also contribute to the likelihood of depression, family violence, and sexual abuse of female children (Subpanel, 1978). They also contribute to a significant emotional and social problem in adolescence: teenage pregnancy (Russo, 1983).

We need to better understand how sex role socialization contributes to the incidence of unintended pregnancy, and develop programs for intervention, particularly for teenagers. The psychological, social, and economic costs associated with teenage pregnancy and childbearing mean that programs and policies designed for prevention of pregnancy in adolescence can have substantial mental health benefits.

Since 1970, more than two out of three firstborn children to teenagers have been conceived by unmarried girls. For black teenagers, the proportion is 90 percent (O'Connell and Rogers, 1984). In 1981, 5 million female adolescents were sexually active and at risk for unintended pregnancy. The limited educational and occupational aspirations of these young girls are major contributing factors in the risk of early pregnancy.

Thus a comprehensive approach to prevention of mental health problems requires addressing issues of male and female sex role socialization and developing programs to promote understanding, respect, and communication between the sexes. It will require examining the predisposing conditions of violence against women, particularly in families, and taking steps to intervene in these conditions. It will require addressing issues of equal rights and opportunities for girls and women in all aspects of society, but particularly in areas of education and employment. For victims of physical and sexual abuse and homeless women, access to housing is also a critical factor in prevention efforts.

Section II

The Agenda

SECTION II.
THE AGENDA

Item 1. Increasing the Visibility and Participation of Women in Leadership Positions in Mental Health Policymaking, Research, Education and Training, and Service Delivery

Although women are entering a broader array of mental health occupations, many problems remain in their move toward equality. Mental health programs and facilities are predominantly administered by men. Male overrepresentation in policy and leadership positions is widespread and can even be found in female-dominated specialties (Russo & VandenBos, 1981).

Although women are the majority in the fields of nursing and social work, these women need leadership training to acquire the essential skills to become more visible and to control resources. For example, a study of program directors of the 1979 training grants of the National Institute of Mental Health revealed that 66 percent of the directors in the predominantly female field of social work were males (Women and Health Roundtable, 1980).

Data collection on the status and career development of women in the mental health profession is a priority. Although some data are available about the numbers of women in the various mental health professions, their salary levels, and their status, much of this information is outdated and not specified by racial and ethnic group. Sex discrimination may arise in recruitment, research opportunities, salary, and promotion procedures. Practices in each of these areas need to be researched, and effective recommendations developed and implemented.

There has been a significant increase in the numbers of women entering the mental health professions that traditionally have been dominated by men. For instance, in 1974, 10 percent of all psychiatrists could be identified as women and 78 percent as men (12 percent could not be identified from the existing data). By 1984, 19 percent were identified as women, 76 percent as men, and 5 percent remained unidentified.

From 1920 to 1974, 22.7 percent of the doctorates in psychology were awarded to women. During the years 1974 to 1982, the percentage increased from 30.8 to 45.5, nearing equality. Subfield segregation has also been reduced, with nearly all subfields in psychology showing an increase in the proportion of women (Russo, 1984b).

A 1978 survey by the American Psychological Association (APA) yielded substantial and pervasive salary differentials between men and women that cut across degree levels and employment settings in psychology and remained after controlling for experience (Russo, Olmedo, Stapp, & Fulcher, 1981). More current data reveal that male psychologists still earn more than females in all of the racial/ethnic groups and across all of the experience levels for which there are sufficient data (National Science Foundation, 1984).

Even the predominately female occupations in the mental health fields show pay inequities. According to the National Association of Social Workers (NASW), in 1982 most female social workers earned between $15,000 to $25,000, whereas most males earned $25,000 or more. The gap was evident throughout the pay range: more than 4 percent of the males earned over $50,000, whereas less than 1 percent of the females earned that much (NASW, 1983).

Information on female psychologists and psychiatrists in academe, where future generations of service providers are educated and trained, indicates persisting patterns of discrimination at the faculty level. Women are substantially underrepresented in U.S. graduate departments of psychology, comprising only 21 percent of the faculty (Russo et al., 1981).

In psychiatry departments at U.S. medical schools, 19.1 percent of the faculty are female (Jolly & Larson, 1976). However, as in departments of psychology, women are more likely to be among the part-time rather than full-time faculty. They are also much more likely to be found in the lower ranks and much less likely to be tenured (Russo et al., 1981). More research is needed to determine why women have a greater tendency to leave their departments before tenure decisions are made and whether they will able to move up from the lower, untenured ranks they now occupy.

There are thus few ethnic minority women in the mental health professions that data on their status are rarely collected and reported. Recent federal budget cuts in support of training in the mental health field may produce substantial decreases in the enrollment of low-income women and minorities. Thus, advances made in increasing the numbers of women in the mental health professions, particularly minority women, may be curtailed or even reversed.

The ability of women to establish a strong presence in the National Institutes of Health (NIH) and the Alcohol Drug Abuse and Mental Health Administration (ADAMHA) is critical for the advancement of women as researchers, policymakers, and role models for future generations of women in the field of mental health. To the extent that women researchers bring a different perspective to research questions, the presence of women at upper-level positions will help shape a research agenda that is more responsive to the full range of women's mental health concerns.

As the number of women receiving doctoral and medical degrees increases, the government must ensure that it successfully recruits a proportionate number of qualified women. It is not currently meeting this objective. For example, the Clinical Associate program at the National Institute of Mental Health (NIMH) is an important training ground for psychiatrists. Yet, over the past five years, only 10 percent of those accepted into the program have been women. In contrast, more than 25 percent of all psychiatric residents since 1976 have been female, and 36 percent were female in 1980 and 1981. Similarly, disappointing recruitment rates are evident in other government mental health programs.

Once women are recruited and hired into a mental health research program, they must produce quality scientific work in order to be retained and promoted. However, the research facilities have a responsibility to provide equal opportunity for all researchers in order to produce the quality work demanded. A range of anecdotal and survey information indicates that women in these programs do not have such opportunities. For example, a 1981 survey of women scientists in the NIMH showed that 62 percent felt that they were excluded from networks in which policy decisions were made and resources allocated (Kafka et al., 1981).

NIH and ADAMHA have very few women in upper-level positions and the rate of promotion for qualified women is substantially lower than that of men, suggesting that a critical eye be placed on the selection systems of mental health programs (Wallis & Frings, 1984; Weiss, Buscher, Shannon, Sample, & Eidskess, 1984). Data on the rates of promotion for men and women in mental health programs are needed. If there is a significant disparity between the sexes, the promotion systems should be examined. Women denied promotions should also be interviewed to ascertain whether there is evidence of individual instances of discrimination.

Of heads of the fifty-four state government mental health programs listed in the directory of the National Association of State Mental Health Program Directors (NASMHPD), only eight are currently headed by women (NASMHPD, 1984). The male overrepresentation in leadership positions on the staffs of mental health programs and facilities is paralleled in the composition of the advisory and governing boards of mental health agencies (cf. Russo & VandenBos, 1981). State government, as well, could benefit from an effort to ensure that qualified female candidates for policymaking positions are not discriminated against in hiring and promotion practices.

Of the fifty-four state government mental health programs, only eight are currently headed by women.

The issue of discrimination against women and minorities is a complex and difficult one to face, particularly in the scientific community whose members see themselves as rational, not as influenced by politics or prejudice. The difficulty in addressing discrimination in the scientific community increases the responsibility to try to bring the issue to the forefront of attention. Mental health policymakers concerned with the future of women in the mental health field must take action to ensure that the recruitment, research opportunities, and promotion procedures at federal and state facilities are free from all vestiges of discrimination.

Item II. Increasing the Knowledge Base About Women's Mental Health, and Ensuring That Sex Bias in Research Does Not Detract From the Quality of that Knowledge Base

Without the development of a knowledge base, improvement in treatment, training, and other areas will be difficult, if not impossible, to implement. There is a need to stimulate the advance of knowledge about women's lives by making research on the mental health implications of women's social and sexual development, work, and family roles a funding priority. Research that identifies strengths as well as problem areas across racial and ethnic groups and stages in the life cycle is particularly needed. Such research should reflect an understanding of the ways that sex bias and sex role stereotyping can affect the research process and detract from the reliability and validity of the results.

Sex bias affects research in obvious and subtle ways, including bias in selection of topics and research participants, in the generalization of findings from males to all persons, and in the formulation of concepts and theories (Task Force on Nonsexist Research, 1981). Inappropriate conclusions about gender differences in mental health and disorder continue to be drawn from studies that are not adequately designed for testing those differences. These conclusions are presented to the public in misleading ways, ways that are potentially harmful because they detract attention from the substantial gender differences in rates and patterns of disorder that exist.

Data from state and federally supported surveys and reporting forms should be collected and analyzed by age, sex, and ethnic group, and across income categories.

Recognition of the importance of addressing issues of sex bias in research is seen in the recent steps that scientific societies have taken to educate their members about these issues. Organizations such as the American Psychological Association, the American Sociological Association, and the Canadian Psychological Association have established groups to develop research guidelines or appropriate educational materials.

More needs to be done. One step, in keeping with the recommendations of the PHS Task Force, is to commission an interdisciplinary panel of senior scientists with expertise in women's issues in research to review existing research and to develop a comprehensive plan for addressing gender bias identified in alcohol, drug abuse, and mental health research.

In addition, data from state and federally supported surveys and reporting forms should be collected and analyzed by age, sex, and ethnic group, and across income categories. As the PHS Task Force recommended, the PHS should take a leadership role by establishing a format for the collection of statistical data on minority population groups so that the needs of ethnic minority women can be assessed.

Although there has been an increasing recognition of the need to design women's programs based on data, there has been a bias toward the use of demographic, epidemiological, and economic data in public policy development. Although these data often suggest the pervasiveness of sex role bias and sex role stereotyping, they do not address issues of the processes involved. Demographic research may be misleading and misinterpreted. A complementary data base of psychological and social research findings is needed so that the causal processes that underlie demographic statistics can be identified and understood.

There has been a bias toward the use of demographic, epidemiological, and economic data in public policy development.

Although understanding women's mental health requires examination of social factors, biomedically-oriented research proposals are more likely to achieve success in the public health service review process than are psychosocial proposals. Policies that affirm the critical importance of research on both biomedical and psychosocial aspects of mental health must be promulgated.

When fewer psychosocial proposals receive funding, mental health researchers are discouraged from applying, creating an even greater decrease of psychosocial research in the area of mental health. Grants for research that specifically targets women's mental health fare even worse. Private foundations have not filled the funding void for women's mental health research and services. Of the $1,792,519,313 expended by private and community foundations in 1984, 1.4 percent went to mental health projects; only .0245 percent went to women's mental health (Clarke, 1984).

A new approach to gender-related psychopharmacology is needed. There is now evidence suggesting that this can only occur by a fuller appreciation of symptoms and treatments within the social and cognitive context of women's lives (Hamilton, in press). Collaboration across disciplines is needed to develop a full picture of how gender relates to mental health over the life cycle. Funding centers for research on gender and mental health over the life cycle could be an effective strategy for increasing the knowledge base about women's mental health.

Item III. Integrating the New Research on Women, Particularly With Regard to Diagnosis and Treatment, Into Mental Health Education, Training, and Practice

The conference participants agreed that how we think about health problems shapes training and research efforts, which in turn shape the nature of the services provided to clients. Women's mental health is affected by women's roles in society, which promote certain behaviors. All treatment efforts must take this basic fact into account. The fundamental priority must be to conceptualize all health problems as being embedded in a social and cultural context.

The same pervasive cultural biases that devalue women and their contributions are found in the training of mental health professionals and in the design and delivery of mental health services (Carmen, Russo, & Miller, 1981; Russo & VandenBos, 1981; Subpanel on the Mental Health of Women, 1978). The new knowledge about women, men, and sex roles has not generally been incorporated into mental health training (Rieker & Carmen, 1983), although the associations representing the mental health professions have recognized the importance of doing so.

Traditional clinical theories of personality specify woman's innate nature as passive, dependent, masochistic, and child-like, and psychological treatment has often aimed at promoting adjustment to the existing order. In an extensive critical review of the literature, Sherman (1980) concluded that "there is a sex-role stereotyping in mental health standards and that sex-role discrepant behaviors are judged more maladjusted." There is also considerable evidence that therapists' knowledge about issues affecting the lives of women is inadequate (Brodsky & Hare-Mustin, 1980). This lack of knowledge is associated with sex bias in therapy (Sherman, Koufacos, & Kenworthy, 1978).

There is also considerable evidence that therapists' knowledge about issues affecting the lives of women is inadequate. This lack of knowledge is associated with sex bias in therapy.

In developing a national agenda to address women's mental health needs, it should be recognized that sex bias and sex role stereotyping affect the delivery of mental health services in paradoxical ways and detract from both appropriateness of and access to treatment (Carmen, Russo, & Miller, 1981; Russo & Olmedo, 1983; Russo & VandenBos, 1981). Women can be considered both overserved and underserved by mental health delivery systems. For disorders congruent with sex role stereotypes, such as depression, conversion hysteria, and phobias, women show higher rates of service utilization than do men. In such cases, issues of appropriateness of services are paramount.

In contrast, problems of women that are congruent with societal views of male domination, such as rape, incest, and physical and sexual abuse, have often been ignored. Similarly, for disorders that are incongruent with society's idealized view of women, such as alcoholism and illicit drug abuse, women's service needs have been neglected. Issues of access to service are central in these latter categories. There is also some evidence that if a man or woman is diagnosed as having a disorder associated with the opposite sex, the likelihood of hospitalization is increased (Rosenfield, 1982).

Funding the development of materials and programs to incorporate the new knowledge about women's lives into the education and training of mental health professionals should be given priority by federal and state policymakers. Service providers must have accurate knowledge about women's development over the life cycle, their work and family roles, and the ways that gender and sex role factors contribute to the etiology, diagnosis, and treatment of mental disorder in diverse ethnic groups.

In addition, service providers must learn an appreciation for the subtle dynamics of sex bias and sex role stereotyping in therapy. The ethical standards that have been adopted by the major professional associations prohibiting sexual intimacy between therapist and client also need to be communicated early in the process of professional socialization. Continuing education programs to supplement present and historical inadequacy in professional training on women's issues are also needed. There are not likely to be any new monies on the federal level, but existing resources can be redirected to serve women better.

Consumer education programs are also important. Mental health professionals should work with the media to develop public education programs. Consumer handbooks such as Women and Psychotherapy (Liss-Levinsen et al., 1985), which is now published by the National Coalition for Women's Mental Health, should be widely disseminated.

There are major questions as to whether assessment techniques and instruments for diagnosing chronic mental illness are appropriate for women. Appropriate diagnosis is critical to effective mental health treatment. The PHS Task Force recommended the review of mental health issues related to women in the next edition of the Diagnostic and Statistical Manual of the American Psychiatric Association. The recent move to define premenstrual syndrome as a psychiatric disorder in the revision of DSM III despite the lack of data on PMS is of particular concern. In addition, a similar mechanism for the review of the International Classification of Diseases should be established.

Graduate and professional training can be enhanced through mechanisms of recruitment, curriculum revision, accreditation standards, and licensure and Board exams. It must also be noted that any discussion of higher education, professional training, and work issues must recognize that early education and socialization are crucial. It is difficult to redirect the stereotypical notions and habits of a young adult entering professional school. A comprehensive approach will require developing coalitions with other fields.

Item IV. Examining and Improving the Impact of Current and Proposed Policies and Programs, Including Financing, on Women's Mental Health Research, Education and Training, and Service Delivery

The PHS Task Force pointed out that relationships among gender, race, economic status, availability of health insurance, use of medical care, and health status warrant continued investigation and programmatic attention. Fragmentation of services and lack of coordination make it difficult to identify gaps in services. The fact that alcohol, drug abuse, and mental health programs and services are often administered in separate programs creates special concerns for women, who are more likely to exhibit multiple problems.

In order to affect training, practice, and research, it is necessary to address structural controls, for example, policy statements, licensure and accreditation, affirmative action, and research review and approval processes. Further, substantial change requires many interventions at multiple points; no single action is sufficient.

Since many of our economic policies have been tailored to the needs of working men, women receive fewer and less generous benefits from such programs as disability insurance, workers compensation, and vocational rehabilitation, where benefit eligibility is tied to participation in the labor force and where benefits correlate with earnings (Kutza, in press). Disabled women earn substantially less than disabled men, are more likely to be unemployed, are less likely to be college-educated, and are less likely to find a job post-disability (Fine & Asch, 1981). In 1982, mean annual earnings for such women who were able to work full-time was $11,979. The comparable figure for disabled men was $21,070 (Russo & Jansen, in press).

The conference participants emphasized the powerful effect that structural factors can have on training, research, and service delivery. The objective of services should be health promotion and disease prevention, not merely the elimination of disease. Whenever possible, the health care system should provide various options and clients should decide what is best for them. Reimbursement must be allowed for a variety of health care providers and for a variety of support services, not just for treatment of diseases by physicians. Clients should have access to the full range of health care workers, and these various professionals should be eligible for third-party reimbursement. Clients should also be apprised of self-help groups that may meet their needs.

As the PHS Task Force pointed out, services such as vocational training, job placement, and child care are more essential for rehabilitating women. Job training and educational counseling that reinforce stereotypes and limit options to lowly paid, traditionally female occupations, such as laundry and housekeeping, are a serious barrier to rehabilitation. Rape counseling and therapy dealing with issues of sexuality are important. In addition, ethnic minority women, particularly those who are poor, experience special stresses and need programs that take their unique concerns into account.

More outreach efforts are needed to make contact with some populations of women who cannot or will not utilize the current system of providing services, such as the chronically mentally ill, disabled, elderly, and homeless. Older and disabled women may need help with transportation in order to better utilize services. Services that take into account the client's language needs, as well as immigrant status, should be provided.

Child care plays a crucial role in ensuring that women have access to treatment, particularly residential treatment (Burt, Glynn, & Sowder, 1979). For example, in one residential drug treatment project, there was an increase of 33 percent in utilization by women clients when residential services for both mothers and children where offered. In another case, utilization by women of a satellite clinic in a multiservice outpatient alcohol project increased from 33 percent to over 50 percent when babysitting services were instituted (Naierman, 1979).

Developing programs to educate the general public about women's mental health problems, available services, and how to select a competent and effective therapist is crucial. Local residents often have minimal knowledge about mental health services offered in their community. Mental health education and consultation that directly focus on the problems of women can increase their ability to handle environmental stress and life crisis (Sobel & Russo, 1981).

Improving the responsiveness of care givers in the community to women's needs can be achieved through both client-centered and consultee-centered case consultation. Caregiver consultation programs can include health professionals, clergy, police, teachers, beauticians, and taxi drivers (Ketterer, Bader, & Levy, 1980). Also needed are efforts to enhance the effectiveness of key human service organizations such as schools, churches, welfare programs, and law enforcement and legal services.

The neglect of women's concerns by the Veterans Administration (VA) deserves special comment. One out of twenty veterans is a woman--nearly 1.2 million women (Russell, 1983). Furthermore, one out of ten members of the current armed forces is a woman, so that the population of women veterans can be expected to grow. Yet, as the recent report of the Veterans Administration Advisory Committee on Women Veterans (1984) concluded, women veterans have not had equal access to medical care and other benefits.

n 1984, of the 16 domiciliaries of the VA medical system, only nine accepted women. Less than one percent of the patients in VA psychiatric facilities are women.

The impact of the VA on mental health research, training, and service delivery goes beyond the veteran population. Service providers and researchers may have their beliefs and expectations about mental disorders shaped by the institutions that train them and the populations they serve. Funding for training and research by the VA reflects VA priorities, priorities that have been oriented toward male patients.

Item V. Developing Prevention Efforts That Will Address the Conflicts and Dilemmas Experienced by Women in Their Families, Work Settings, and Communities

The conference participants discussed the issues faced by women in families and in work settings where bias and discriminatory practices have a negative impact on women's mental health. Participants underscored the critical importance of incorporating gender issues into prevention efforts. Prevention requires changing societal institutions and norms that create conflicts and dilemmas for women, reinforce their powerlessness and devalued status, and increase their risk of poverty. Educational efforts designed to promote self-confidence, autonomy, and status in girls and women are necessary to promote their mental health.

In addition, policymakers in education, the media, business, labor, housing, finance, and other fields must all be involved in changing the societal institutions that create stress and conflicts that are destructive to mental health.

Although there have been significant changes in women's roles and status in recent years, sex bias and discrimination still pervade the American family structure and work environment. Almost without exception women are charged with the responsibility for housework and child care. Even among working couples without children, women spend nearly twice as many hours as men do on household duties (Denmark, Shaw, & Ciali, in press). Employed women are left to their own devices to find appropriate child care while, at the same time, balancing the demands of job, home, and motherhood. The costs of child care for single-parent families headed by women are so great that many of these women are unable to participate in the labor force.

Despite the role conflicts faced by working mothers and the added economic burden of child care, most employers do not provide child care for their employees. The availability of quality day care has not matched the dramatic increase in the number of employed women. Since 1940 the number of employed women has more than tripled, but the number of employed mothers has increased more than ten times. In 1982, 59 percent of all mothers with children under 18 years of age were in the labor force. (Russo & Jansen, in press). The most recent labor force statistics indicate that almost half of the married mothers of children one year old or younger are employed outside of the home.

Women's increased educational status and participation in the labor force has not significantly altered their disadvantaged economic status. Women still earn approximately 60 cents for every dollar that men earn. College-educated women earn about the same as men who are high school drop-outs--$12,085 and $11,936, respectively (Russo, 1984).

Lower wages and a benefits structure based on earnings increases the likelihood of poverty for women at all ages. It is estimated that if women were paid the same wages that similarly qualified men earn, the number of families living in poverty would be cut in half (Pearce & McAdoo, 1981).

Despite the passage of the Equal Pay Act in 1963, women have not achieved pay equity. There is evidence that sex differences in skill level and job experience are not responsible for women's lower pay. For example, women with years of experience in traditionally female occupations such as secretary and child care worker, earn less than parking lot attendants and dog pound attendants, occupations that require less education or skills but are most frequently occupied by men. The National Academy of Sciences (NAS) has concluded that women whose positions are different than the positions of men are paid less, despite the comparability of those positions. Furthermore, the NAS found that the more an occupation is dominated by women, the less that occupation will pay (Hartman & Treiman, 1981).

An additional problem for single mothers, is the lack of enforcement of child support payments. A study by the Commission on the Economic Security of Women found that only 26 percent of single mothers received some support for alimony or child support (Gregory & Kaplan, 1983). In 1982, more than one out of three female-headed households were in poverty (Gregory & Kaplan, 1983). Single mothers are therefore more likely to go without the necessities of adequate food, clothing, and shelter.

This economic burden produces tremendous anxiety and engenders a sense of frustration and hopelessness that frequently leads to depression. As a result, single mothers are more likely to report the need for professional help to deal with psychological problems.

Women represent 63 percent of all persons below the poverty level who are over 15 years of age.

Given this situation, basic reforms in protection of women's rights can be considered critical for primary prevention of mental health problems. Passage of the Equal Rights Amendment (ERA) is a necessary, although not sufficient condition for ameliorating the disadvantages of women's economic and social status that undermine mental health. In the absence of the ERA, legislation that ensures equal access to education and job training becomes critical. This legislation does not require additional funds--but it would help ensure that both sexes have equal opportunity to share in the benefits of the programs that are funded.

Legislation promoting sex equity in education and in programs receiving federal financial assistance has had important implications for mental health. Unfortunately, recent decisions by the Supreme Court have eroded legal protections in these areas.

Title IX of the Education Amendment has been a key statutory provision for eliminating sex discrimination in education. It has covered all aspects of educational institutions, including regulations dealing with counseling, health services, marital and parental status, and physical education and athletics. Furthermore, the Supreme Court held that Title IX created a private right of action for the victims of illegal discrimination, thus opening a new area for litigation.

Title IX has offered an important tool for addressing discriminatory policies and practices in our educational institutions, including those directly in the domain of mental health professionals. Legislation ensuring that Title IX covers the total institution even though only one program may receive federal funds is crucial for creating environments of equal opportunity in our educational systems.

In addition, a comprehensive approach to promoting mental health and preventing mental illness requires examining the predisposing conditions of violence against women, particularly in families, and taking steps to intervene in these conditions. There is a rape every six minutes. Mental health professionals must be concerned with the impact of this crime on the victim. The impact of this crime goes beyond the victim, however. Even if a woman does not experience rape, the possibility can affect her choices and opportunities. Mental health professionals must work with the criminal justice system in addressing these issues.

Section III

Reports
of the
Working Groups

SECTION III.
REPORTS OF THE WORKING GROUPS

Group I: Gender Bias in Mental Health Education and Training, Theories, Research, and Practice

Facilitator: Bonnie Strickland, Ph.D.
Rapporteur: Jacquelyn H. Hall, Ph.D.
Participants: Jeannette Chamberlain, R.N., Ed.D.
                              Ruth Kahn, M.S., R.N.
                              Joyce Kobayashi, M.D.
                              Delores Parron, Ph.D.
                              Stanley Schneider, Ph.D.

Issues/Priorities

1. The women's movement is relatively inactive with regard to women's mental health issues. Key efforts have been made by women's groups in the mental health professions, however, even these groups have lost their momentum on policy issues in recent years.

2. Greater sensitivity has developed in the mental health professions. Unfortunately, as a result of less active federal encouragement of affirmative action, within Initial Review Groups fewer questions about gender issues or female role models are raised in reviews of proposals for training programs.

3. Professional training and curricula dealing with women's issues--particularly within clinical disciplines--are not being given sufficient priority.

4. New knowledge about the psychology of women is not systematically included in the training experience of health professionals. There is a desperate need for this kind of information in professional education as well as in-service programs for staff development.

5. To make matters worse, resources for continuing education programs, which are needed to supplement present and historical inadequacy in professional training on women's issues, are shrinking.

6. Understanding women's mental health requires examining social factors. However, within most Public Health Service agencies, biomedically-oriented research proposals are more likely to receive funding than are psychosocial proposals.

7. Medical education is a prime example of successful institutional change. In recent years one-third of the first-year students in medical schools have been women. The experience of today's medical students, therefore, is quite different from the experience students had 15 years ago when women were 8 percent of the class. There have been few corresponding changes, however, in the compositions of medical school faculties or in the curricula related to women.

8. Women are entering a broader array of occupational fields, both in clinical and research areas, and there is a resulting decrease in some fields that traditionally have had larger proportions of women. Nonetheless, women still are concentrated in the "social concern" areas, and these are devalued.

9. There appears to be a "feminization" in the human service sector, particularly within clinical disciplines, for many men now are going into business and technical fields that are more financially profitable. This has severe long-term implications for status and pay within the human service sector.

10. While enrollment is dropping in the women-intensive service fields of social work and nursing, entrepreneurial interests are increasing. Fee-for-service organizations that contract for nursing care exemplify the trend. Institutions that are likely to suffer most from this phenomenon are the public hospitals, which may take on even more of a "dumping ground" quality than they have now.

11. There is a need for leadership training programs, particularly within those programs that are women-intensive, such as nursing and social work. Although women are well-trained in those fields and are the majority of professional persons, when it comes to interdisciplinary interaction, they are not found in leadership roles that enable them to achieve more visibility and to control resources.

12. There are relatively few women in the administrative hierarchy of mental health enterprises in government, service facilities, or academic institutions.

Recommendations

1. We would like for this conference to be an instrument for revitalizing advocacy for women's issues in mental health. Although this discussion group has focused on higher education,

professional training, and work issues, we realize that early education and socialization are crucial. It is difficult to redirect the stereotypical notions and habits of a young adult entering professional school.

2. On issues of early socialization, the mental health professions must form coalitions with other fields such as education.

3. In order to affect training, practice, and research, it is necessary to address structural controls such as policy statements, licensure and accreditations, affirmative action, and research review and approval processes. Further, substantial change requires many interventions at multiple points; no single action can make a big difference.

4. Graduate and professional training can be enhanced through mechanisms of recruitment, a more developmental and lifespan approach to mental health curricula, accreditation standards, and licensure and Board exams.

5. Information about the mental health of women and minorities needs to be systematically included in all training for health professionals. Perhaps the most effective strategy is to aim toward changes in the structural controls. For example, as soon as there is a cluster of questions on licensure and board exams that relate to women's mental health, graduate training curricula will change quickly to accommodate the new demand.

6. Within the DHHS there are not likely to be any new monies, so existing resources must be redirected to serve women better. Implementation of recommendations from the Public Health Service Task Force on Women's Health can be accomplished by redirecting existing resources to ensure that women are studied appropriately and are included in funding mechanisms.

7. Women's interest groups must contact and visit agency heads within the Public Health Service to ask for action and a timetable for accomplishing certain goals. Women must use collegial networks in the "corridors of power" to influence the allocation of resources and to advocate for programs and the advancement of women in organizational leadership.

8. Special opportunities must be considered for women, not only designing new programs, but also channeling women into existing programs such as the NIH Clinical Associate Program or other kinds of fellowships and specialized training assignments.

9. Leadership training for women should be set in place, particularly in the women-intensive fields.

10. Perhaps the nursing research that is supported through the Health Resources and Services Administration could be expanded to include mental health.

11. In order to help women get into executive positions, it is essential that they have support by professional organizations and by congressional representatives.

12. Affirmative action statements should be included in grant program announcements as a visible affirmation of the federal interest in fostering women's participation.

Important Areas of Research and Services

1. Large groups of women who have worked for most of their lives are retiring. These women have different interests and life patterns than do women who have been homemakers for most of their lives. We do not yet know what influence that will have on the lives of older women, but we do feel that the group of energetic recent retirees are a valuable resource for work on women's issues.

2. Women experience a ubiquitous stress that is different from that experienced by men. As a group, women face more economic stress and discrimination, and women always face potential sexual victimization. Research is warranted to determine if this stress may contribute to women's greater susceptibility to autoimmune diseases such as multiple sclerosis and lupus.

   In addition, there is a challenge to be made on the matter of post-traumatic stress disorder: Thousands of women are victimized each year through physical and sexual abuse, but their post-trauma experience is not addressed on a large scale. However, men who experience post-traumatic stress disorders from the Vietnam combat have received services and compensation nationwide.

3. The bereavement process for women bears more attention, because women typically outlive men. More and more women are working outside the home when they lose their male partners, but there are no structures in the workplace culture to help women through the grieving process as they maintain their jobs.

4. There is a need for attention to mental health aspects of health problems that are predominant in women, such as arthritis, reproduction- related disease, and disorders of old age.

Group II: Women in the Family, at Work and in the Community

Facilitator: Patricia Perri Rieker, Ph.D.
Rapporteur: Mary Jansen, Ph.D.
Participants: Florence Denmark, Ph.D.
                     Carol Nadelson, M.D.
                     Nancy Reame, Ph.D.
                     Nancy Sharp, M.S.N.
                     Diana M. Zuckerman, Ph.D.

General Statement

The most often cited problems for women are related to economic status. To promote optimal mental health, we need to pay special attention to the areas of child support, child care, the growth of single-parent families, and the feminization of poverty. We must also develop and implement a research, training, and political agenda to address the specific recommendations of this conference.

Issues/Recommendations

1. New Definition of the Family

   We firmly encourage the broad dissemination of a new definition of the family. This new definition should include the concept of two or more people living together in a committed relationship. Examples of a committed relationship include single-parent families, lesbian and gay families and relationships, extended families, and nuclear families.

2. Career and Personal Issues

   a. We must develop "freedom of information" about career paths. Career ladders need to be genuine ladders for women, whereby women have real access to top positions.

   b. Personal characteristics such as gender, physical handicap, ethnic group, and sexual preference should not be used to deny opportunity in employment or career advancement.

3. Child Care/Dependent Care

   a. We need additional research into the link between mental health and role conflict relating to work and family. Stress is produced as a result of role conflicts in decisions to have children, to remain at home with those children, and to return to work. We need new and innovative ways to assist and support women with these decisions and responsibilities.

b. We encourage legislation that will reduce role strain by providing incentives for the care of family members, including children and disabled or dependent adults. This is a "pro-family" position.

c. It is essential that there be child care in the work place. We must provide incentives to employers to establish child care programs to reduce role conflict.

d. We need better dissemination of research findings on the benefits to children and families of alternative child care arrangements.

4. Uniform Child Support and Custody

a. We encourage federal legislation to provide nonsexist child custody, and we support policies that are uniform across states.

b. We encourage research on alternative child custody models, including joint custody.

c. We strongly support enforcement of child support payments.

d. We encourage mediation rather than adversarial solutions to custody and support decisions.

e. Sexual orientation should not be a factor in child care or custody decisions.

5. Mental Health Implications of Reproductive Choices

a. We encourage research into the mental health implications of various reproductive choices such as adoption, surrogate parenting, and in vitro and in vivo fertilization.

b. We must ensure that women are appointed to those decision-making bodies that influence ethical decisions in reproductive care, such as the National Commission on the Ethics of Biotechnology.

c. We must encourage the growth of health care delivery that promotes women's mental health through research and program development in facilities such as birthing centers.

6. Pay Equity/Comparable Worth

a. We support enforcement of pay equity legislation.

b. We encourage passage of legislation for comparable worth.

7. Political Skill Development

   a. We support collective action by women in areas in which mental health is at stake, especially actions such as lobbying and electing candidates to political office.

   b. Some specific strategies to accomplish this include meeting with women in congressional office, organizing within our own associations, and establishing coalitions with other groups.

   c. We must teach women to be effective politically by using the power of our numbers in the legislative and political process.

8. Legislation

   a. We strongly support speedy passage of the Equal Rights Amendment to promote the autonomy and the mental health of American women.

   b. We strongly support the speedy passage of the Civil Rights Act of 1985. This legislation would discourage discrimination on the basis of sex, race, religion, age, and disability.

   c. We support federal and state legislation to facilitate the transition of AFDC mothers into the work force by making job training available and by providing food stamps and Medicaid to the working poor.

   d. We oppose legislation that limits reproductive freedom, including bills that restrict family planning by cutting funding for organizations such as Planned Parenthood. We oppose the proposed constitutional amendments that would make abortion and some forms of contraception illegal. In addition, we oppose legislation that would limit access to abortion for poor women, racially and ethnically diverse groups, and federal employees.

   e. We encourage the federal government to make legislative commitments to welfare programs and to health care for families. The federal government should do much more to assist with dependent care of children, elderly parents, and single-parent families. Economics should not determine levels of health care or mental health care. We need a rational, ethical means to deliver quality health care to all citizens.

9. Diversity in Ethnicity, Culture, and Socioeconomic Status

The issues addressed by this group are mediated by cultural, ethnic, class, immigration status, and linguistic group factors. Problems, solutions, and strategies addressed by this group should systematically consider these issues and ensure the representation of the diversity of women in our society.

10. Proposal for a National Women's Mental Health Organization

We propose the formation of a national women's mental health organization to expand and implement the conference agenda. It should have an interdisciplinary and ethnically diverse steering committee that will develop a structure and organize the implementation efforts. The steering committee will also secure funds to ensure the success of this endeavor. An initial priority will be to begin dialogue with key congressional leaders whose support is needed to move the conference agenda.

Group III: Diagnosis and Treatment

Facilitator:	Mildred Mitchell-Bateman, M.D.
Rapporteur:	Angela McBride, Ph.D.
Participants:	Hortensia Amaro, Ph.D.
	Barbara Claster, Ph.D.
	Nina Feldman, Ph.D.
	Jean A. Hamilton, M.D.
	Joan Medway, M.S.W.
	Dorothy Miller, M.S.W.

General Statement

The conceptualization of health problems shapes both training and research efforts, which in turn shape the nature of the services provided to clients. Women's mental health is affected by women's roles in society, which promote certain behaviors; all treatment efforts must take this basic fact into account.

Issues/Priorities

The fundamental priority must be to conceptualize all health problems as being in a context, that is, a socioeconomic, cultural, generational, developmental, or lifestyle context. If care is to be provided within a contextual framework, the following factors must be taken into account:

1. Reimbursement must be allowed for a variety of health care providers and for a variety of support services, not just for treatment of diseases by physicians.

2. Provision of child care should be considered a basic service to clients.

3. Services should be provided that take into account a client's language needs, as well as immigrant status.

4. Job training and educational counseling should not limit occupational training for women to lowly paid areas that are stereotyped as female, such as laundry and housekeeping.

5. Services to the client should be coordinated so that the total person can be served. Case management should not follow the medical model, which underscores the supremacy of the physician.

6. Clients should have access to the full range of health care workers, and these various professionals should be eligible for third-party reimbursement. Clients should also be apprised of self-help groups that may meet their needs.

7. Both health promotion and disease prevention should be the objective of services, not merely the elimination of disease.

8. The health care system should provide various options, and clients should be apprised of their options in deciding what is best for them.

9. On entry into the health care system, a developmental history should be taken, so that health care providers can understand the person within the context of his or her background. Specifically, the professional should inquire about whether the person has ever been subject to abuse, since so many chronic psychiatric patients have this area as part of their history.

10. Every attempt should be made to ensure that the treatment itself does not create more health problems, that is, iatrogenic disease. For example, drug therapy can have disastrous side effects; sexual abuse may be a feature of some counseling situations.

11. The stigma attached to some health care problems such as alcoholism, and to seeking help must be taken into account in treatment efforts. This effort involves working closely with the media.

12. The prejudices of health care providers, such as gender stereotyping and linguistic bias, must be taken into account in treatment efforts.

Two examples of problems that need to be considered within a contextual framework are depression and obesity. Women receive a disproportionate amount of anti-depressant drugs. Although women appear to be over-medicated, the first two phases of drug screening typically avoid using women as subjects. Women in their twenties, thirties, and early forties are systematically excluded from drug research because they are in the childbearing years, but this population is the very one that is most likely to suffer from depression. Since women are less responsive to the anti-depressants on the market and are more likely to be troubled by side effects, a reconceptualization of depression that takes into account socioeconomic, cultural, generational, developmental, and lifestyle issues is needed in order to treat them appropriately.

Obesity is another problem that exists in a complicated context. Body image concerns trouble the majority of women; they also have a different proportion of muscle to fat that affects their metabolism. Since each round of dieting depresses the metabolism further, dieting as a treatment may create more problems than it resolves. Dieting may even encourage binge-eating.

Two other problems were identified. We need more data generally about women's mental health problems, services provided to them, and the consequences of existing treatments. This need is particularly urgent in the area of ethnic minority women.

Existing data collection does not provide much information about the factors affecting the mental health of minority women, particularly with regard to the etiology, diagnosis, and treatment of mental disorder. National and state data on certain ethnic groups are unavailable due to the inadequacy of ethnic identifiers in health surveys and reporting forms that are required and utilized by federal and state agencies.

Developing appropriate ethnic identifiers in health and mental health data surveys and reporting forms was seen as an urgent priority. Data should be reported by gender and ethnic group in order to allow analysis of the problems and needs of ethnic minority women. In addition, research is needed on appropriateness of services, effectiveness of existing treatment, and ethnic-specific factors that affect the mental health of ethnic minority women, such as immigration and acculturation.

Finally, women are likely to have multiple problems requiring multiple diagnoses. Different health care problems are treated separately, and as a result women become overmedicated. This is particularly a problem for elderly women. The situation is made worse by the fact that sexual stereotypes shape diagnoses.

Recommendations

The group urged that all concerned with women's mental health monitor existing legislation for the mental health component. Fuller use for women should be made of existing entitlements, such as the Older American Act with its Mental Health Amendment and Social Security disability insurance. Four general strategies were proposed:

1. The major one was the establishment of a national coalition for women's mental health. It would bring together organizations and individuals concerned with women's mental health. Since there is no existing research center that focuses on women's mental health, such a coalition would encourage research in that area, for example, through collaborative studies. This organization would serve as a clearinghouse for resources and information, for example, by coordinating conferences and developing a videotape exchange.

It might be innovative in the area of service by encouraging the development of demonstration projects. It would serve an advocacy function and work on such issues as selection of a woman for the currently available position of Deputy Director of the National Institute of Mental Health. It would also be concerned about curriculum development, possibly putting together model curricula. It would influence the media, perhaps by issuing fact sheets or a series of "true stories" with upbeat solutions to current concerns.

2. The second strategy involves becoming more effective at the state level. For example, we should ensure that each state department of mental health has a person or task force concerned with women or that each commission on the status of women has a mental health component. Every effort should be made to sensitize both commissioners of mental health and state offices of policy management to women's mental health concerns.

3. The third strategy involves lobbying relevant federal agencies to devise better ethnicity identifiers for all data gathered at state and federal levels. All relevant agencies should be requested to conduct data analysis and reporting of health and mental health status by gender and ethnicity. These identifiers should be reported in a systematic fashion in separate yearly reports and integrated into all health and mental health data reports.

4. Finally, FDA should confront the problems created when women are not part of the first two stages of the clinical testing of new drugs. It is also important that male animals not be used exclusively in the development phase before studies with humans are conducted.

Group IV: Physical, Sexual, and Psychological Abuse*

Facilitator: Elaine Carmen, M.D.
Rapporteur: Linda S. King, M.S.W.
Participants: Irene Hanson Frieze, Ph.D.
                          Dorothy Harris, M.S.W.
                          Susan W. Talbott, R.N., M.A., M.B.A.

Issues/Priorities

1. There is a need for recognition and identification of the problem and its parameters and effects. The reason is that females, as adults and as children, are exposed to many multiple forms of physical, sexual, and psychological violence by virtue of their subordinate status, the social power differential between women and men, women's status as sexual objects, and the acceptance of violence as a norm in our culture.

2. Victims are blamed and held responsible for the violence. Prevention requires structural change.

3. There are cause-and-effect dynamics in terms of chronicity, generational dynamics, and long-term effects that link abuse to mental illness.

4. Special populations such as poor women, lesbians, the chronically mentally ill, handicapped/disabled women, and adolescent mothers are more vulnerable to violence.

5. Sexual abuse of female clients by mental health and health professionals needs to be addressed.

6. It should be a routine and standard procedure as part of intake/assessment protocols in institutions and private practice to determine the presence of violence and victimization experiences in a client's life.

7. Coordination and collaboration of service providers is inadequate. What is needed is a multidisciplinary involvement of criminal justice, law enforcement, social service, health, mental health, and grass roots or self-help groups.

8. The power of the media should be used constructively to highlight the problems and interventions.

---

*Spouse abuse, peer abuse, child abuse, incest, elder abuse, rape, sexual exploitation including pornography, sexual harassment in both the work and social setting, and personal/property crimes.

9. Government needs to be influenced to utilize its resources and make legislative changes and reforms, including policy formulation.

10. There is a need for improving and changing the response of the criminal justice system. We should strive for uniformity of legislation and for federal as opposed to state legislation. An example of improved response would be expanding victim compensation.

11. Prevention and treatment programs are needed.

12. Both basic and applied research is needed on the effects of victimization on women in particular; treatment and intervention techniques; chronicity of abuse and its effects on women; long-term coping mechanisms of abused women; and the "feminization" of victimization, including the societal view of victims and its impact on the victimization experience.

Recommendations:

Females, as adults and as children, are exposed to multiple forms of physical, sexual, and psychological violence by virtue of the social power differential between them and males, their status as sexual objects, and the general acceptance of violence as a norm in our culture. Therefore, those social factors that contribute to violence against women must be remediated as part of preventing the victimization of women.

1. Education and Training

   a. Training related to violence against women, its causes, treatment, and intervention, should be required in the theory and practica of all professional schools.

   b. Continuing education programs should include credit for workshops, training, and courses on violence against women.

   c. Education and training of mental health professionals should take place in professional organizations and associations, on the school level, and through the development of a flexible, generic curriculum package based on existing curricula that would include a bibliography and a list of resources.

   d. Funding for the curriculum package should be sought through NIMH and through local level sources.

2. Research

    a.   Existing resources should be used. It would be helpful to publicize and disseminate information on research money through professional organizations' newsletters, conventions, and other appropriate vehicles.

3. Service Delivery

    a.   Experienced professionals in the field should be encouraged to continue contributing through direct service provision.

    b.   A national conference on service delivery for female victims of violence should be held. It should include interdisciplinary representation that allows for integrating models for treatment and intervention.

    c.   The issue of access to a sufficient quality and quantity of services, especially for the poor, should be addressed at a national conference.

    d.   A priority should be the provision of immediate sanctuary or shelter to victims of abuse.

4. Prevention and Consumer Awareness

    a.   Early education should take place in the schools.

    b.   The new prevention arm at NIMH for program funding needs to be used.

    c.   Parent education should take place in day care centers and in other appropriate institutions.

    d.   Media education could be aided by awards for good reporting or journalism from the mental health professional organizations.

    e.   Work with local groups, such as the Junior League, should be collaborative and supportive, as they are sources for funding and volunteers.

    f.   Employee assistance programs should be utilized for consumer awareness and prevention.

5. Public Policy

    a.   Passage of ERA should continue to be a priority.

    b.   There is a need to target existing and pending legislation and implement new legislation to influence the provision of resources for women victims.

    c.   Legislation that is a barrier to the development of the full rights of women should be changed.

    d.   There is a need to be proactive in scrutinizing, assessing, and monitoring legislation and regulations that have an impact on the victimization of women. The appropriate vehicles are the professional organizations.

6. Target/Approach Funding Agencies

    a.   Employers need to be approached regarding the cost of absenteeism and increased health benefit costs for employees because of violence against women. Groups such as Catalyst, which has corporate leaders on its board, should be included.

    b.   The prevention arm of NIMH should be approached as a potential funding source.

    c.   On the local level, an attempt should be made to match the interests of individual enterprises with the issue of victimization of women. An example is Levi Straus's funding of shelters in cities that house their distribution centers.

7. Creating Networks

    a.   We need to hold a national conference that builds on the work of this planning conference and focuses on service delivery issues and dissemination of operational models for treatment of and intervention with women victims.

Group V: Chronically Mentally Ill Women*

Facilitator: Ellen L. Bassuk, M.D.
Rapporteur: Carol T. Mowbray, Ph.D.
Participants: Lillian Comas-Diaz, Ph.D.
          Margaret Hastings, Ph.D.
          Diane K. Kjervik, M.S., R.N., J.D.
          Nancy Lane-Pales, Ph.D.
          Nancy E. Taylor, B.A.

General Statement

The chronically mentally ill have been recognized nationally as a high priority treatment group. However, sex differences have barely been considered. In fact, most writing on the chronically mentally ill suggests that they are seen as being genderless. But, to the extent that differences have been identified through experience, anecdote, or in some case studies, the results suggest that chronically mentally ill women have different and more extensive problems than do men, whereas treatment is basically designed to be male-oriented. All the problems discussed in the other work groups are worse for this population group.

In discussing the needs of chronically mentally ill women, the following subpopulations need to be identified:

● The aging with mental disorders,

● Young chronically mentally ill women,

● Midlife women, particularly with regard to chronic problems of mentally ill with marginal skills,

● Homeless single females,

● Homeless women with children,

● Chronically mentally ill women in community programs,

● Institutionalized women,

● Women with dual diagnosis of mental illness and substance abuse,

● Women with dual diagnosis of mental illness and developmental disabilities.

---

*In using the label chronically mentally ill, we are ascribing to the definition used in the National Plan for the Chronically Mentally Ill, which focuses on a severe level of disability in a number of major life areas that occurs on an intermittent or continuous basis.

The most prominent content areas to be addressed to meet the needs of chronically ill women are:

- Physical and sexual abuse in the family (current and past history),

- Sexual abuse/harassment,

- Roles in the family and the community, such as mothers, workers, and wives,

- Housing,

- Health,

- Medication.

Homeless women are a special population of concern. The work group's focus on this group is not meant to imply that all the homeless are chronically mentally ill. However, it is believed that a greater proportion of individual homeless women than of homeless men have serious psychopathology, often combined with substance abuse, and that the numbers of individual homeless women are increasing. For homeless families, there are significant safety issues, for example, mothers and their small children are likely targets for physical and sexual abuse.

The work group wished to bring attention to a special issue, that of women as caretakers. Most mentally ill persons who are cared for by their families are cared for by wives, mothers, or sisters. This group deserves special consideration.

Issues/Priorities

1. The major issue that must be addressed is the lack of an adequate knowledge base. The work group felt that a lot has been learned over the past 8 to 10 years about chronically mentally ill persons, but relatively little was known about sex differences. We do not know to what extent chronically mentally ill women's needs and problems are different from men's. Until this information base is established, improvements in treatment, training, and other areas will be difficult, if not impossible, to implement. There is a particular dearth of information and controlled studies on homeless mentally ill females and no studies on homeless mentally ill families.

2. A second area of concern involves assessment and measurement issues. Are the assessment techniques and instruments for diagnosing a chronic mental illness appropriate for women, so as to pick up significant social dysfunction in major life areas at an early point in their disorders? For example, women may be as dysfunctional as men are in their roles and behavior, but they do not create as much disturbance, and so are not identified.

Research indicates that chronically mentally ill and schizophrenic women are older than men. Is this because there is a later onset for women or because women do not come to public attention until late in their disorders when a less reversible condition has been established?

3. A third major concern is that of treatment. The chronically mentally ill need long-term care, and they often have multiple problem areas that require multiple service deliverers. The mental health sector cannot meet all the needs. To do so will require bringing together mental health and social service systems to meet basic human needs like shelter, food, and income maintenance. In addition, there must be important connections with the several health care systems and the legal system.

The following list of treatment needs applies to the chronically mentally ill without regard to gender. Where specific needs of women have been identified, we have noted these. Otherwise, we simply do not know the specific extent and nature of women's problems compared to men's.

a. Availability of child care, support for mothering role, skill training regarding motherhood;

b. Protection and safe environment--women are usually more vulnerable as victims;

c. Outreach services--women do not respond to and are isolated from traditional services;

d. Family planning information, contraceptive availability, appropriate sexuality training--women with mental disabilities are often sexual victims (willing and unwilling) or are sexually harassed;

e. Basic social skills training, such as community living, socialization, assertiveness, or prevocational;

f. Financial--women are less often eligible for SSDI because they do not have a job history, and are not eligible for VA benefits;

g. Case managers (CMs) are needed who are trained around women's issues. For women with families, CMs have to extend themselves more into other service systems;

h. Asylum and sanctuary--we do not have the techniques to rehabilitate some subpopulations (we do not know the percentage). They will need life-long asylum and sanctuary;

i. Prescribed psychotropic medications--indications, dosage, drug interactions, polypharmacy, side effects. There are special concerns for pregnant women and those with menstrual irregularities;

j. Substance abuse--alcohol and prescription, street, and over-the-counter drugs;

k. Dual diagnosis--this population often slips through the cracks because they are shuffled around from one system to another. This is a special problem for women because they are more likely to be prescribed medications and to combine them with alcohol.

l. Housing--stepwise, graded, supervised or semi-independent living; safe environments and providing a range of options, especially for families. Often professionals assume that the best post-hospitalization placement is in the family home, but chronically mentally ill women often have a history of incest and physical abuse from their families as well as battering (physical and mental) from their spouses;

m. Vocational rehabilitation--women are not given as much vocational preparation as males or are trained for traditional female occupations for which employment is less likely and pay levels lower;

n. Health (medical assessment and care)--women have more chronic health conditions, especially because chronically mentally ill females are older than males.

4. The fourth major issue is that of training. Public institutions (community mental health centers and state hospitals) need to create programs to attract professionals and paraprofessionals and to develop their interest in working with chronically mentally ill women. More people must be well trained, and traditional training programs have not met this need.

In addition, physicians need more appropriate training on the use of psychotropic medications and their continued monitoring. This is especially an issue for chronically mentally ill women because the majority of CMI persons are on medication, and physicians tend to overmedicate women.

Recommendations

1. Increasing Awareness and Developing a Knowledge Base

   a. Issue a special RFP with significant funding available for services and epidemiological research on chronically mentally ill women and with special attention paid to the homeless, elderly, minority, and young adult populations. Because of their complex and specialized nature, the proposals should be reviewed by a special review panel, composed of at least 50 percent women, with expertise on the CMI and services research.

   b. Develop training tracks in the care disciplines that focus on the CMI, and include curriculum on special women's issues.

   c. Any HHS report or policy statement on the CMI must address gender differences.

   d. Chronically mentally ill women do not have access to appropriate services. In the ADAMHA block grant, the current set-aside money (10 percent for unserved/underserved populations) should be targeted for demonstration and evaluation projects specifically for CMI women through the new regulations for block grants issued by HHS.

2. Policy and Financing

   Women make up the majority of older adults with severe mental health problems. Because services in nursing homes and in the community are inadequate for older adults, we recommend the following:

   a. Medicare should change discriminatory policies on financing appropriate services to the CMI, lift the 190-day lifetime inpatient limitation on psychiatric hospitalization, and improve and expand outpatient services.

   b. Medicaid should carefully reexamine the Institutions for Mental Diseases Rule for how it discourages appropriate diagnosis and treatment programs in nursing homes, reform policies so that more money consistently goes to community-based services for CMI persons, and continue to explore private long-term care financing. The program should encourage the development of long-term care insurance to cover chronic mental illness.

3. Treatment and Services Issues for CMI Women

    a. Treatment planning for CMI women must include attention to family planning, access to contraception, and sexuality training.

    b. There should be adequate public support for safe 24-hour shelter facilities for women that provide necessary services and for transitional housing facilities.

    c. Shelters should provide intensive case management services with pediatric consultation to homeless families.

    d. There must be capacity in the mental health system to diagnose mental health problems in the geriatric population (age 60 and over).

    e. Casefinding, outreach, referral, and treatment capacities to deal with the mental health problems of the homeless are necessary.

    f. Inappropriate psychotropic drug treatment continues to be an issue for CMI women. This must be addressed through training, monitoring, and treatment efforts.

    g. We must have a full range of services available and accessible to serve the CMI women, including emergency/crisis assistance, residential alternatives, respite, intensive treatment, clinical/diagnostic, outpatient, rehabilitation, socialization, and assessment and maintenance services such as income maintenance.

    h. Mechanisms for increasing community awareness and acceptance of the CMI are necessary to ensure that housing in the community is available and in acceptable locations in order to ensure safety and access to services for women.

    i. Special attention needs to be given to identifying and treating chronically mentally ill ethnic/minority women, since families tend to deny the problem and attempt to "take care of them" themselves. We need services that take into account different languages, values, and cultures.

    j. CMI women need low-cost housing. If decent and safe low-cost housing does not exist in a community, these women will be homeless.

k. There is a need to reassess financing mechanisms, such as Medicare, Medicaid, and SSI, with regard to treatment of CMI women. The aim should be to ensure that the full range of services are provided, with special attention given to unifying health and social services.

l. There should be an examination of the impact of commitment laws with emphasis on alternatives to care for women who do not fit commitment criteria, e.g., guardianship.

m. We are not advocating reinstitutionalization. But unless the full range of services is established, hospitals will be increasingly used. Because schizophrenia is a chronic, relapsing illness, short-term hospitalization is necessary. In addition, a small percentage of patients will require long-term hospital beds.

n. Primary prevention strategies should be developed for women's mental health problems, so that chronic mental disability is not an outcome. Better research is needed on this subject so that model programs and high risk groups may be identified and cost-effective approaches implemented.

Group VI: Special Populations

Facilitator: Carolyn R. Payton, Ed.D.
Rapporteur: Reiko Homma True, Ph.D.

Participants: Johanna Ghe-e-bah Clevenger, M.D.
                                          Jane Delgado, Ph.D.
                                          Susan Gore, Ph.D.
                                          Barbara N. Logan, Ph.D.
                                          Caitlin Ryan, M.S.W.
                                          Eva Stewart, M.S.W.

General Statement

While the needs and problems of special populations are complex and extensive, little attention has been given to identifying and understanding them by policy makers, governmental organizations and professional groups. Information about the following groups is particularly needed: adolescents, mid-life women, elderly women, minority women, lesbians, poor women, women with disabilities, lower class women, rural women, women veterans, and women in prisons. Although some research and data have begun to accumulate in recent years among various professional groups, dissemination of this information is difficult because of the lack of information-sharing mechanisms crosscutting the boundaries of those professional disciplines.

Among mental health professionals there is general recognition of the significant level of problems that exist for these special populations, but the resources available to address these problems are extremely meager or often inappropriate. While a group of committed grass-roots people have demonstrated some success in developing alternative programs to address the needs of the special populations, they are systematically excluded from government support when these strategies are legitimized by government funding agencies.

Issues/Priorities

1. Children and Adolescents

The Committee recognized that there are many emerging issues dealing with children and adolescents such as teen suicides, homeless youth, abused children, teenage pregnancy, and substance abuse. However, we felt that Group II will have a more significant role in dealing with these issues. Some issues identified by us as not likely to be identified by other groups were:

a.   Current policies and practices dealing with the child welfare, e.g. adoption or foster home placement.

b. Native American and lesbian mothers are treated particularly punitively by various agencies and professional groups.

c. There is a need to re-examine and revamp, if appropriate, potentially deleterious practices.

2. Mid-life women

While Group II is likely to be addressing mid-life women's concerns, Group VI felt the need to underscore the following issues:

a. Many women in mid-life transition face stressful and often traumatic events such as divorce, separation, and loss of significant family members. Despite their need for much professional and program support, only limited resources are available to these women.

b. As more women enter the world of high-pressure professions, there is an emerging trend among them to become victims of alcoholism and drug abuse. Although they are still not very visible, an effort should be made to develop resources and support for them. Included among them should be minority women.

3. Elderly Women

The group was particularly concerned about the increasing difficulties imposed on elderly women and their families in dealing with their care. Current reimbursement practices by health care and social service agencies are punitive toward anyone attempting to provide home care. The responsibility is frequently placed on women, often daughters, who are in the mid-life stage. However, little support, either psychological or financial, is available to help them deal with the problems.

Elderly women from minority cultures, particularly those a with monolingual background, have difficulty locating culturally appropriate resources. Alternatives such as use of other elderly women or culturally sensitive groups or nursing homes should be encouraged.

Other issues identified were:

a. Prevalence of poverty;

b. Deinstitutionalized women;

c. Dealing with the loss of spouses;

d. Isolation from the community, especially in developing and rural communities;

e. Abuse of prescription medication;

f. Inadequate coverage of health care costs by various funding resources;

g. Proposed Medicare DRG system may further limit women's access to health care.

4. Minority Women

Issues identified were:

a. Problems faced by immigrant women;

b. Dual and triple pressures of dealing with work, family, and racism/sexism;

c. Problems created by generational differences;

d. Adjustment difficulties, including the pressures created by differential rate of adjustment with their spouses;

e. Increased incidence of abuse by their spouses.

5. Lesbians

Issues identified were:

a.. Need for more information on lesbian mental health;

b. Lack of opportunity for publication of information on lesbian mental health issues;

c. Punitive laws and regulations dealing with such critical issues as employment, child custody, and other civil rights;

d. Limited social support network, since lesbians are often alienated from families of origin;

e. Special strains on lesbians of color;

f. Scapegoating in academia of those doing teaching and training on lesbian issues;

g. Limited curriculum on lesbian issues.

6. Women Veterans

Issues identified included:

a. Lack of visibility within the military and veterans' organizations;

b. High incidence and risk of sexual abuse for women in the military;

c. Persecution of lesbian veterans;

d. Unavailability of services for women, e.g., gynecological services, inpatient beds, substance abuse services;

e. Limited staffing of women veterans to provide support and counseling to women Vietnam veterans;

f. Exclusion of women vets from pertinent areas of research such as post traumatic syndrome and Agent Orange;

g. Violence against women married to men in the military;

h. Access to pensions, particularly as it affects divorced wives of military personnel;

i. Wives of career military men whose opportunity for their own career development was neglected because of frequent movement;

j. War brides, especially Asian women.

Recommendations

1. Children and Adolescents

a. Professional and governmental agencies' current policies and practices dealing with lesbian or Indian mothers and children should be re-examined and new strategies developed.

b. An effort should be made to support and coordinate with organizers of the International Year of Youth.

2. Mid-Life Women

a. We should advocate for the identification and needs assessment of issues faced by mid-life women.

b. The funding agencies, both governmental and private, should be approached to develop support and funding for programs serving the needs of mid-life women including those of displaced homemakers, professional women in distress, and minority women.

3. Elderly Women

a. We should advocate with federal, state, and professional organizations to develop funding and technical support for older women's programs, including culturally appropriate alternative programs.

b. We should urge reexamination of current health care policies and practices relative to the care of elderly women.

4. Minority Women

We should urge identification of needs among minority women, particularly dealing with the unique and multiple problems they face and advocate for development of support programs.

5. Lesbians

a. Mental health organizations and other related institutions should be urged to develop solid and unbiased information regarding the diversity of women's lives in their training programs.

b. They should include pre-professional and professional programs, continuing education, practica, professional schools, text books, and licensing and certification.

6. Women Veterans and Military Wives

a. We should urge the VA and DOD to support the funding of research endeavors by women's groups on issues dealing with women veterans and women in the military.

b. We should advocate with VA, DOD, and other federal legislative groups to support development of programs staffed by personnel sensitive to the needs and issues of women veterans and wives of military personnel.

c. We should advocate for the funding and staffing of programs designed to prevent and treat sexual abuses among women in the military. Programs such as the one developed by American Lake (Tacoma) VA Hospital should be recognized as a model for other areas.

d. We should advocate for the development of relevant curriculum dealing with military women's issues in professional schools, officer training, and service academies.

e. We should support the education and training of military wives so that they can become self-sufficient.

7. Special Populations in General

a. We should take an active role in encouraging federal, state, and professional organizations to support data collection and information dissemination on issues faced by the special populations.

b. We should urge the professional organizations to advocate for the expansion of the educational and training content in each of their disciplines to include special population-related issues.

c. We should urge the relevant federal, state and professional organizations to support funding for research into issues faced by the special populations.

d. We should urge the appropriate government and private funding agencies to support financing of services targeted for the special populations.

e. We should reaffirm the need for affirmative action in education, training and employment, thus assuring the participation of women representing special populations.

f. In advocating for program, training, and research development, a provision should be made to assure representation of target populations in the process.

g. We should reaffirm the need for the feminist perspective to insure freedom of bias against women in all endeavors.

h. We should urge the U.S. government to ratify the U.N. Convention resolution regarding the elimination of all forms of discrimination against women.

Section IV

References

SECTION IV.
REFERENCES

American Psychiatric Association. (1984). The homeless mentally
ill. Washington, DC: Author.

Armitage, K. J., Schneiderman, L. J., & Bass, R. A. (1979).
Response of physicians to medical complaints in men and women. Journal
of the American Medical Association, 241, 2186-2187.

Bachrach, L. (1984). Deinstitutionalization and women. American
Psychologist, 39, 1171-1177.

Bassuk, E. L., Rubin, L., & Lauriat, A. (1984). Is homelessness a
mental health problem? American Journal of Psychiatry, 141, 1546-1550.

Baxter, E., & Hopper, K. (1982). The new mendicancy: Homeless in
New York City. American Journal of Orthopsychiatry, 52, 393-408.

Belle, D. (1980). Who uses mental health facilities? In
M. Guttentag, S. Salasin, & D. Belle (Eds.), The mental health of women.
New York: Academic Press.

Belle, D. (Ed.). (1982). Lives in stress: Women and depression.
Beverly Hills, CA: Sage.

Brodsky A. M., & Hare-Mustin, R. (Eds.). (1980). Women and
psychotherapy: An assessment of research and practice.
New York: Guilford Press.

Burt, M. R., Glynn, T. S., & Sowder, B. J. (1979). Psychosocial
Characteristics of Drug-Abusing Women. Washington, DC: U.S.
Department of Health, Education, and Welfare.

Carmen, E. H., Russo, N. F., & Miller J. B. (1981). Inequality and
women's mental health: An overview. American Journal of Psychiatry,
138, 1319-30.

Castelli, J. (1984, October). Curbs on religious actions.
The Cult Observer, 1 (3) 5.

Center for Women's Policy Studies. (1984, January/February).
Response. Washington, DC: Center for Women Policy Studies, 9.

Cicchinelli, L. F., Belle, J. C., Dittmar, N. D., Manzanares, D. L.,
Sackett, K. L., & Smith, G. (1981, April). Factors influencing the
deinstitutionalization of the mentally ill: A review and analysis. Denver,
CO: University of Denver, Denver Research Institute.

Clarke, K. (1984). Focus: Grants for women and girls. The Foundation Grants Index Bimonthly. New York: The Foundation Center.

Cooperstock, R. (1978). Sex differences in psychotropic drug use. Social Science and Medicine, 12B, 179-186.

Cottler, L. B., & Robins, L. (1983). The prevalence and characteristics of psychoactive medication use in a general population study. Psychopharmacology Bulletin, 19, 746-751.

Crandall, V. C. Achievement behavior in young children. (1967). In W. W. Hartup & N. L. Smothergill (Eds.), The young child. Washington, DC: National Association for the Education of Young Children.

Cuskey, W. R., Berger, L. H., & Densen-Garber, J. (1977). Issues in the treatment of female addiction: A review and critique of the literature. Contemporary Drug Problems, 6, 307-371.

Cypress, B. K. (1980). Characteristics of visits to female and male physicians: The national ambulatory medical care survey, 1977. Hyattsville, MD: National Center for Health Statistics.

Davis, L. J., & Brody, E. M. (1979). Rape and older women: A guide to prevention and protection. Washington, DC: U.S. Department of Health and Human Services, National Center for the Prevention and Control of Rape.

Denmark, F. L., Shaw, J. S., & Ciali, S. D. (in press). The relationship between sex roles, living arrangements, and the division of household responsibilities. Sex Roles.

Department of Justice, Federal Bureau of Investigation. (1984). Uniform crime reports for 1983. Washington, DC: U.S. Goverment Printing Office.

Department of Health & Human Services. (1984a). Helping the homeless: A resource guide. Washington, DC: Author.

Department of Health & Human Services. (1984b). The homeless: background, analysis and options. Washington, DC: Author.

Department of Housing & Urban Development. (1984). A report to the Secretary on the homeless and emergency shelters. Washington, DC: Author.

Department of the Navy, Office of Naval Research. (1983). Department of the Navy family advocacy program: service need and service response. Arlington, VA: Department of the Navy.

Depp, F. C., & Ackiss, V. (1984, April). Meeting the social and psychiatric needs of sheltered women. Paper presented at the meeting of the American Orthopsychiatric Association, Toronto, Canada.

Dobash, R. E., & Dobash, R. (1979). Violence against wives: A case against the patriarchy. New York: Free Press.

Dweck, C. S., Davidson, W., Nelson, S., & Enna, B. (1978). Sex differences in learned helplessness: II. The contingencies of evaluative feedback in the classroom and III. An experimental analysis. Developmental Psychology, 14, 268-276.

Dweck, C. S., & Gilliard, D. (1975). Expectancy statements as determinants of reactions to failure: Sex differences in persistence and expectancy change. Journal of Personality and Social Psychology, 32, 1077-1085.

Entwisle, D. R., & Baker, D. P. (1983). Gender and young children's expectations for performance in arithmetic. Developmental Psychology, 19, 200-209.

Fidell, L. S. (1981). Sex differences in psychotropic drug use. Professional Psychology, 12, 156-162.

Fine, M., & Asch, A. (1981). Disabled women: Sexism without the pedestal. Journal of Sociology and Social Welfare, 8, 233-248.

Gatz, M., Fuentes, M., & Pearson, C. (n.d.). Health and mental health of older women in the 1980's: Implications for psychologists. University of Southern California, Los Angeles, Department of Psychology.

Glynn, T. J., Pearson, H. W., & Sayers, M. (Eds.). (1983). Women and drugs. Research Issues 31. (ADM 83-1268). Washington, DC: U.S. Government Printing Office.

Gove, W., Hughes, M., & Style, C. B. (1983). Does marriage have positive effects on the psychological well-being of the individual? Journal of Health and Social Behavior, 24, 122-131.

Guttentag, M., & Salasin, S. (1976). Women, men, and mental health. In L. A. Carter & A. F. Scott (Eds.), Women and men: Changing roles, relationships, and perceptions. New York: Aspen Institute.

Guttentag, M., Salasin, S., & Belle, D. (Eds.). (1980). The mental health of women. New York: Academic Press.

Halbreich, U., Asnis, G., & Goldstein, S. (1984). Sex differences in response to psychopharmacological interventions in humans. Psychopharmacology Bulletin, 20, 526-530.

Hamilton, J. A. (in press). Guidelines for avoiding methodological and policymaking biases in gender-related health research. Report submitted to the Public Health Service Task Force on Women's Health.

Hamilton, J. A., Alagna, S. W., & Sharpe, K. (in press). Cognitive approaches to the evaluation and treatment of premenstrual depression. In H. Osofsky (Ed.), Washington, DC: American Psychiatric Association.

Hamilton J. A., & Conrad, C. (in press). Toward a developmental psychopharmacology: The physiological basis of age, gender, and hormonal effects on drug responsivity. In J. Call (Ed.), Handbook of child psychiatry.

Hamilton, J. A., Lloyd, C., & Alagna, S. W. (1984). Gender, depressive subtypes and gender-age effects on antidepressant response: Hormonal hypotheses. Psychopharmacology Bulletin, 20, 475-480.

Hamilton, J. A., & Parry, B. (1983). Sex-related differences in clinical drug response: Implications for women's health. Journal of the American Medical Women's Association, 38, 126-132.

Hartman, H. I., & Treiman, D. J. (Eds.). (1981). Women, work, and wages. Washington, DC: National Academy Press.

Herman, J. L. (1981). Father-daughter incest. Cambridge: Harvard University.

Herrington. L. H. (1985). Victims of crime: Their plight, our response. American Psychologist, 40, 99-103.

Hilberman, E. (1980). Overview: The "wife-beater's wife" reconsidered. American Journal of Psychiatry, 137, 1336-47.

Homeless Youth Steering Committee. (1984). Meeting the needs of homeless youth. Albany, NY: New York State Council on Children and Families.

Horgan, C. M. (1982, November). A comparison of utilization and expenditure patterns for ambulatory mental health services in the specialty mental health and the general medical sector. Paper presented at the meeting of the American Public Health Association, Montreal, Canada.

Hughes, R., & Brewin, R. (1979). The tranquilizing of America: pill popping and the American way of life. New York: Harcourt Brace Jovanovich.

Jolly, H. P., & Larson, T. A. (1976, March). Participation of women and minorities on U.S. medical faculties. Washington, DC: U.S. Department of Health and Human Services, Bureau of Health Manpower.

Kafka, M. S., Davenport, Y., Gold, P., Susman, E., Tallman, J., Waxler, C., & Yang, H-Y. (1981, February). Interim report of the ad hoc committee to evaluate the differential impact of the NIMH intramural program on men and women. Washington, DC: National Institute of Mental Health.

Ketterer, R. F., Bader, B. C., & Levy, M. R. (1980). Strategies and skills for promoting mental health. In R. H. Price, B. C. Bader, & J. Monahan (Eds.), SAGE annual reviews of community mental health: Vol. 1. Prevention and mental health: research, policy, and practice. Beverly Hills, CA: Sage.

Kimmel, D. C. (1974). Adulthood and aging: An interdisciplinary developmental view. New York: Wiley.

Kinney, J., Trautmann, J., & Gold, J. A. (1981). Underrepresentation of women in new drug trials. Annals of Internal Medicine, 95, 495-499.

King, L. S. (1981, May/June). Responding to spouse abuse: The mental health profession. Washington, DC: Center for Women Policy Studies.

Klerman, G. L., & Weissman, M. M. (1980). Depressions among women: Their nature and causes. In M. Guttentag, S. Salasin, & D. Belle (Eds.), The mental health of women. New York: Academic Press.

Kutza, E. (in press). Benefits for the disabled: How beneficial for women? Sociology and Social Welfare.

Lear, J. G. (1983). Women's health and public policy: 1976-1982. In I. Tinker (Ed.), Women in Washington: Advocates for Public Policy (pp. 148-162). Beverly Hills, CA: Sage.

Lennane, K. J., & Lennane, R. J. (1981). Alleged psychogenic disorders in women--A possible manifestation of sexual prejudice. The New England Journal of Medicine, 95, 495-499.

Levine, I. S. (1984). Homelessness: Its implications for mental health policy and practice. Psychosocial Rehabilitation Journal, 8, 6-16.

Liss-Levinson, N., Clamar, A., Ehrenberg, M., Ehrenberg, O., Fidell, L., Maffeo, P., Redstone, J., Russo, N. F., Solomons, H., Tennov, D. (1985). Women and psychotherapy: a consumer handbook. Tempe, AZ: National Coalition for Women's Mental Health.

Maccoby, E. E., & Jacklin, C. N. (1974). The psychology of sex differences. Stanford, CA: Stanford University Press.

Moore, E. C. (1980). Women and health. Washington, DC: U.S. Government Printing Office.

Naierman, N. (1979). Sex discrimination in health and human development services: A final report to the Office of Civil Rights, Division of Planning, Budget and Research. (Contract No. HEW-100-78-0137). Cambridge, MA: ABT Associates, Inc.

National Association of Social Workers. (1983). Membership survey shows practice shifts. NASW NEWS, 28.

National Association of State Mental Health Program Directors. (1984, December). Roster of directors and commissioners. Washington, DC: Author.

National Institute on Alcohol Abuse and Alcoholism. (1983). Alcohol and women. (DHEW Publication No. ADM 80-835). Washington, DC: U.S. Government Printing Office.

National Institute on Drug Abuse. (1983). Women and drugs (Research Issue No. 31). Washington, DC: U.S. Department of Health and Human Services.

National Science Foundation. (1984). Women and minorities in science and engineering. Unpublished data.

Parry, H. J., Balter, M., Mellinger, G., Cisin, I., & Manheimer, D. (1973). National patterns of psychotherapeutic drug use. Archives of General Psychiatry, 28, 769-783.

Pearce, D., & McAdoo, H. (1981). Women and children, alone and in poverty. Washington, DC: National Advisory Council on Economic Opportunity.

Raskin, A. (1974). Age-sex differences in response to antidepressant drugs. Journal of Nervous and Mental Disorders, 159, 120-130.

Regier, D. A., Myers, J. K., Kramer, M., Robins, L. N., Blazer, D. G., Hough, R. L., Eaton, W. W., & Locke, B. Z. (1984). The NIMH epidemiological catchment area program. Archives of General Psychiatry, 41, 934-941.

Rieker, P. P., & Carmen, E. H. (1983). Teaching value clarification: The example of gender and psychotherapy. American Journal of Psychiatry, 140, 410-415.

Rieker, P. P., & Carmen, E. H. (Eds.) (1984). The gender gap in psychotherapy: Social realities and psychological processes. New York: Plenum Press.

Rix, S. E. (1984). Older women: The economics of aging. Washington, DC: Women's Research and Education Institute of the Congressional Caucus for Women's Issues.

Rodino, P. (1985). Current legislation on victim assistance. American Psychologist, 40, 104-112.

Rosenfield, S. (1982). Sex roles and societal reactions to mental illness: The labeling of "deviant" deviance. Journal of Health and Social Behavior, 23, 18-24.

Russell, M. S. (1983). The female veteran population. (RSM 70-84-1). Washington, DC: Office of Reports and Statistics, Veterans Administration.

Russo, N. F. (1984a). Women in the American Psychological Association. Washington, DC: American Psychological Association.

Russo, N. F. (1984b). Women in the mental health delivery system: Implications for policy, research, and practice. In L. Walker (Ed.). Women and mental health policy. Beverly Hills, CA: Sage.

Russo, N. F. (in press). Sex role stereotyping, socialization, and sexism. In A. Sargent (Ed.), Beyond sex roles (rev. ed.). St. Paul: West Publishing Company.

Russo, N. F. & Jansen, M. (in press). Women, work, and disability: Opportunities and challenges. In A. Asch & M. Fine (Eds.), Disabled women: Psychology from the margins.

Russo, N. F., & Olmedo, E. L. (1983). Women's utilization of outpatient psychiatric services: Some emerging priorities for rehabilitation psychologists. Rehabilitation Psychology, 28, 141-155.

Russo, N. F., Olmedo, E., Stapp, J. & Fulcher, R. (1981). Women and minorities in psychology. American Psychologist, 36, 1315-1363.

Russo, N. F., & Sobel, S. B. (1981). Sex differences in the utilization of mental health facilities. Professional Psychology, 12, 7-19.

Russo, N. F., & VandenBos, G. R. (1981). Women in the mental health delivery system. In W. H. Silverman (Ed.), Community mental health: A sourcebook for board and professionals and advisory board members. New York: Praeger.

Russo, N. F. (June, 1983). Psychological aspects of unintended pregnancy and abortion. Testimony presented to the Subcommittee on Health and the Environment Committee on Energy and Commerce, United States House of Representatives, Washington, D.C.

Seidler, S. (1984, March/April). Drug use and the elderly. Network News. (Available from the National Women's Health Network, Washington, DC).

Sherman, J. A. (1980). Therapist attitudes and sex-role stereotyping. In A. M. Brodsky, & R. Hare-Mustin (Eds.), Women and psychotherapy. New York: Guilford Press.

Sherman, J. A., Koufacos, C., & Kenworthy, J. A. (1978). Therapists: Their attitudes and information about women. Psychology of Women Quarterly, 2, 299-313.

Smith, C. A., & Smith, C. J. (1980). Learned helplessness and preparedness in discharged mental patients. Social Work Research and Abstracts, 14, 21-27.

Sobel, S. B., & Russo, N. F. (Eds). (1981, February). Sex roles, equality, and mental health. Professional Psychology, 22 (Whole No. 1).

Stein, L., Del Gaudio, A. C., & Ansley, M. Y. (1976). A comparison of female and male neurotic depressives. Journal of Clinical Psychology, 32, 19-21.

Subpanel on the Mental Health of Women. (1978). Report to the President, Volume III (pp. 1022-1116). Washington, DC: U.S. Government Printing Office.

Task Force on Nonsexist Research. (1981). Guidelines for nonsexist research. Washington, DC: The American Psychological Association, Division 35.

Tavris, C., & Baumgartner, A. I. (1983, February). How would your life be different? Redbook, pp. 92-95.

Test, M. A., & Berlin, S. B. (1981). Issues of special concern to chronically mentally ill women. Professional Psychology, 12, 136-145.

Thurer, S. (1983). Deinstitionalization and women: Where the buck stops. Hospital and Community Psychiatry, 34, 1162-1163.

Veroff, J., Kulka, R. A., & Douvan, E. (1981). The inner American: Self-portrait from 1957-1976. New York: Basic Books.

Veterans Administration Advisory Committee on Women Veterans. (1984). Report of the Veterans Administration Advisory Committee on Women Veterans. Washington, DC: Author.

Walker, L. (Ed.). (1984). Women and mental health policy. Beverly Hills, CA: Sage.

Wallen, J., Waitzkin, H., & Stoekle, J. D. (1979). Physician stereotypes about female health and illness. Women and Health, 4, 135-146.

Wallis, L. A., & Frings, J. (1984, February). National Institutes of Health gender staffing patterns. New York: Regional Council for Women in Medicine, Inc.

Weiss, S., Buscher, M., Shannon, R., Sample, K., & Eidskess, P. (1984, September). Alcohol, Drug Abuse and Mental Health Administration Women's Council Report to the Administrator: 1983-1984. Washington, DC: U.S. Department of Health and Human Services.

White House Mini-Conference on Older Women. (1981). Growing numbers, growing force: A report from the White House Mini-Conference on Older Women. Des Moines, IA: Author.

Whitman, J. R., & Duffy, R. (1961). The relationship between type of therapy received and a patient's perception of his illness. Journal of Nervous and Mental Disorders, 133, 288-292.

Women and Health Roundtable. (1980). 4 (2), 1-3.

Women's Task Force. (1982). For better or for worse? Women and the mental health delivery system. Lansing, MI: Michigan Department of Mental Health.

Women's Task Force. (1983). Special populations: Problems and perspectives. Lansing, MI: Michigan Department of Mental Health.

Zuckerman, Diana M. (1985). Confidence and aspirations: Self-esteem and self-concepts as predictors of students' life goals. Manuscript submitted for publication.

Section V

Conference Advisory Committee

SECTION V.
CONFERENCE ADVISORY COMMITTEE

LEONA BACHRACH, PH.D., Research Professor of Psychiatry, Maryland Psychiatric Research Center, University of Maryland School of Medicine; served as staff sociologist for the President's Commission on Mental Health, coordinating both the Task Panel on Deinstitutionalization, Rehabilitation, and Long-Term Care, and the Task Panel on Rural Mental Health.

ELAINE CARMEN, M.D., Visiting Professor of Psychiatry, Harvard Medical School, Massachusetts Mental Health Center, and Visiting Research Scholar, Wellesley College, Center for Research on Women; Professor of Psychiatry, University of North Carolina School of Medicine; former Director, Psychiatric Inpatient Unit, North Carolina Memorial Hospital; Member, Subpanel on the Mental Health of Women, President's Commission on Mental Health; former Chair, Committee on Women, American Psychiatric Association; Member, Task Force on the Curriculum of the Psychology of Women and Men, American Psychiatric Association. Co-chair, National Coalition for Women's Mental Health.

BARBARA L. CLASTER, PH.D., Private practice, New York City; Coordinator of Women's Issues, Postgraduate Center for Mental Health; Chair, Task Force on Gender Issues, New York City Psychotherapy Training Institutes; Chair, Task Force on Clinical Training and Practice, Division of the Psychology of Women, American Psychological Association; Member, Steering Committee, Feminist Therapy Institute; Moderator, Women's Issues Study Group, American Orthopsychiatric Association; Chair, Task Force on Mental Health of Women, jointly sponsored by the Advisory Committee for Mental Health and Mental Retardation of the Pennsylvania Department of Public Welfare, and the Pennsylvania Commission for Women; Executive Committee, National Coalition for Women's Mental Health.

FLORENCE L. DENMARK, PH.D., Thomas Hunter Professor in the Social Sciences, Hunter College and the Graduate Center, City University of New York; former President of the American Psychological Association (APA); former Chair, Committee on Women in Psychology, APA; incoming member, Committee on Gay Concerns, APA; former President, Division of the Psychology of Women, APA; former President, New York State Psychological Association; Board of Trustees, Association for the Advancement of Psychology; Executive Committee, National Coalition for Women's Mental Health.

RHETAUGH G. DUMAS, PH.D., Dean, School of Nursing, University of Michigan; former Deputy Director, National Institute of Mental Health, Alcohol, Drug Abuse and Mental Health Administration; Charter Fellow, American Academy of Nursing; American Nurses' Association; American Black Nurses' Association; American Public Health Association.

MARGARET HASTINGS, PH.D., Executive Director, Commission on Mental Health and Developmental Disabilities, State of Illinois; Government Policy and Professional Advisory Committees of National Mental Health Association; National Health Policy Committee of the American Health Planning Association; Member and former Chair of the Illinois Title XX Council; Executive Committee, National Coalition for Women's Mental Health.

NANCY A. HUMPHREYS, D.S.W., Director, School of Social Work, Michigan State University; past National President, National Association of Social Workers; President's Advisory Committee on Women, Carter Administration; Advisory Committee on (Legal) Professional Ethics, Supreme Court of the State of New Jersey; Commissioner, Los Angeles County Commission on Children's Institutions; Supporting Member, New Jersey Association of Hispanic Human Services Professionals; Board member, National Conference on Social Welfare.

MARY JANSEN, PH.D., Dean for Professional Affairs, California School of Professional Psychology; Member, Council of Representatives, American Psychological Association (APA); Chair, Committee on Women, Division of Health Psychology, APA; Chair, Continuing Education Committee, World Federation for Mental Health; Member, Subcommittee on Disability, National Mental Health Association; Editor, Rehabilitation Psychology; Executive Committee, National Coalition for Women's Mental Health.

JEAN BAKER MILLER, M.D., Clinical Professor of Psychiatry, Boston University School of Medicine; former Director, Stone Center for Developmental Services and Studies, Wellesley College; Principal faculty, NIMH Staff College Course on Mental Health Services for Women; Board of Directors, Elizabeth Stone House; Past Chair, Committee on Women, Massachusetts Psychiatric Society.

CAROL MOWBRAY, PH.D., Director, Innovations Division, Michigan Department of Mental Health (DMH); Vice-Chair, Executive Committee, State Mental Health Program Directors; Chair, Women's Issues Task Force (DMH); Committee on Women, Division of Psychologists in Public Service, American Psychological Association; Planning Committee, Michigan Mental Health Association.

NAOMI NAIERMAN, Chair, Women's Mental Health Agenda Project Advisory Committee; Past Chair, Women and Health Roundtable; former Deputy Director, Abt Associates; Project Director, NIMH Survey of Community Mental Health Center Clients; Author Sex Discrimination in Health and Human Development Services.

CAROLYN R. PAYTON, Ed.D., Dean of Counseling and Career Development, Howard University; former Chair, Committee on Women in Psychology, American Psychological Association (APA); former member, APA Task Force on Sex Bias and Sex-Role Stereotyping in Psychotherapeutic Practice; Member, Board of Psychologist Examiners, District of Columbia; Member, Commission on the Homeless, District of Columbia; winner of APA's Distinguished Service Award; Executive Committee, National Coalition for Women's Mental Health.

NANCY FELIPE RUSSO, PH.D., Director of Women's Studies and Professor of Psychology, Arizona State University; first Administrative Officer, Women's Programs Office, American Psychological Association, Washington, D.C.; Project Director, National Women's Mental Health Agenda Conference; former President, Federation of Organizations for Professional Women; Chair, Mental Health Advisory Committee, Women and Health Roundtable and former Member of the Steering Committee; Member, Subpanel on the Mental Health of Women, President's Commission on Mental Health; Member, Long-Term Research Committee, Women's Research and Education Institute of the Congresswomen's Caucus; Chair, National Coalition for Women's Mental Health.

JEANNE SPURLOCK, M.D., Deputy Director, American Psychiatric Association; and former member of the Subpanel on the Mental Health of Women of the President's Commission on Mental Health.

BONNIE STRICKLAND, PH.D., Professor of Psychology and former Associate to the Chancellor, University of Massachusetts; former Chair, Board of Professional Affairs, American Psychological Association; former Chair, Council of Graduate Departments of Psychology; President, Division of Clinical Psychology, APA; Member, National Advisory Council on Mental Health; Member, Council of Representatives, APA; President-elect, American Psychological Association (1985); Executive Committee, National Coalition for Women's Mental Health.

REIKO HOMMA TRUE, M.S.W., PH.D., Area Deputy Director for Adult Services, San Francisco City and County Community Mental Health Services; Vice Chair, Committee on Women in Psychology, American Psychological Association (APA); Chair, Task Force on Asian Women, Division of the Psychology of Women, APA; Board of Directors, Asian American Psychological Association; Member, Quality Assurance and Minority Services Committees, California State Psychological Association; Treasurer, Asian Women United.

Section VI

Conference
Participants

SECTION VI.
CONFERENCE PARTICIPANTS

ELOISE MOORE AGGER, D.S.W., Private practice in psychoanalytic psychotherapy; Member, Board of Directors and former President, D. C. Institute of Mental Hygiene, Washington, D.C.; Clinical Trainer, Child Welfare Project for High Risk Families, University of Minnesota, former Project Director and Field Instructor, Internship and Children of Battered Women Treatment Program, House of Ruth emergency shelters; Assembly Delegate, National Association of Social Workers.

HORTENSIA AMARO, PH.D., Assistant Professor of Pediatrics, Boston University School of Medicine; Research Psychologist, Child Development Unit, Boston City Hospital; former Project Director, Alcohol Research Center, Neuropsychiatric Institute, UCLA; Founding Member, National Hispanic Psychological Association; Chair-elect, Committee on Women in Psychology, American Psychological Association; Member, Health Task Force, Governor's Commission on Hispanic Affairs, Commonwealth of Massachusetts; Executive Committee, National Coalition for Women's Mental Health.

ELLEN L. BASSUK, M.D., Associate Professor of Psychiatry, Harvard Medical School; Assistant Psychiatrist, Beth Israel Hospital, Boston; Governor's Advisory Committee on the Homeless, Commonwealth of Massachusetts; former Science Fellow, Bunting Institute, Radcliffe College; Committee on Deinstitutionalization, Massachusetts Association for Mental Health; Chair, Chronic Mental Illness Subcommittee, Health Policy Research and Education Institute, Kennedy School of Government, Harvard University.

ELISSA BENEDEK, M.D., Clinical Professor of Psychiatry, Wayne State University; Director, Training and Research, Center for Forensic Psychiatry; Consultant, National Institute for Mental Health, Problems of In-patient Women; Fellow and Vice-President, American Psychiatric Association; former Chair, Committee on Women, American Psychiatric Association; Member, Committee on Women, Michigan Society of Neurological Psychiatry; Council Member, American Academy of Child Psychiatry.

LAURA S. BROWN, PH.D., Clinical Assistant Professor of Psychology, University of Washington, Seattle; Private practice of psychotherapy; Member, Steering Committee, Feminist Therapy Institute; member, Committee on Women in Psychology, American Psychological Association; former National Conference Coordinator, Association for Women in Psychology; Host, Laura Brown Show, KVI Radio, Seattle, Washington.

---

*Member, Conference Advisory Committee

CAROL E. BURROUGHS, M.A., Conference Coordinator, Women's Programs Office, American Psychological Association; Candidate for the J.D. Degree, Catholic University of America; former Contract EEO Investigator, Department of Housing and Urban Development and the U.S. Department of Agriculture; former Technical Expert, Student Sexual Harassment Prevention Training Project, U.S. Department of Education Contract; former National President, Women's Equity Action League; former Equal Opportunity Specialist, Wayne State University, Detroit, Michigan.

ELAINE CARMEN, M.D.*, Visiting Professor of Psychiatry, Harvard Medical School, Massachusetts Mental Health Center, and Visiting Research Scholar, Wellesley College, Center for Research on Women; Professor of Psychiatry, University of North Carolina School of Medicine; former Director, Psychiatric Inpatient Unit, North Carolina Memorial Hospital; Member, Subpanel on the Mental Health of Women, President's Commission on Mental Health; former Chair, Committee on Women, American Psychiatric Association; Member, Task Force on the Curriculum of the Psychology of Women and Men, American Psychiatric Association. Co-chair, National Coalition for Women's Mental Health.

JEANNETTE CHAMBERLAIN, R.N., ED.D., Chief, Psychiatric Nursing Education Program, Division of Human Resources, National Institute of Mental Health, Alcohol, Drug Abuse, Mental Health Administration, Department of Health and Human Services; former Associate Professor/Director, Psychiatric Nursing Programs, University of Washington, Seattle, Washington; Member, Council of Nurse Researchers, American Nursing Association; Member, Executive Committee, Federally Employed Women.

BARBARA L. CLASTER, PH.D.*, Private practice, New York City; Coordinator of Women's Issues, Postgraduate Center for Mental Health; Chair, Task Force on Gender Issues, New York City Psychotherapy Training Institutes; Chair, Task Force on Clinical Training and Practice, Division of the Psychology of Women, American Psychological Association; Moderator, Women's Issues Study Group, American Orthopsychiatric Association; Chair, Task Force on Mental Health of Women, jointly sponsored by the Advisory Committee for Mental Health and Mental Retardation of the Pennsylvania Department of Public Welfare, and the Pennsylvania Commission for Women; Member, Steering Committee, Feminist Therapy Institute; Executive Committee, National Coalition for Women's Mental Health.

JOHANNA GHE-E-BAH CLEVENGER, M.D., Private practice, Dallas, Texas; Attending Physician, Baylor University Medical Center; Minority Representative, Assembly of the American Psychiatric Association; President and Founding Member, Association of American Indian Physicians; Board of Directors, Dallas Intertribal Center; Member, Committee on Women, Texas District Branch, American Psychiatric Association.

LILLIAN COMAS-DIAZ, PH.D., Administrative Officer, Ethnic Minority Affairs, American Psychological Association, Washington, D.C.; former Assistant Professor of Psychology, Department of Psychiatry, Yale University, New Haven, Connecticut; former Director, Hispanic Clinic, Connecticut Mental Health Center.

JANE DELGADO, PH.D., Senior Health Policy Coordinator, immediate Office of the Secretary, Health and Human Services, Washington, D.C.; responsible for ADAMHA, NIMH, NIAAA, NIDA, block grants and special populations; private practice, Washington, D.C.

FLORENCE DENMARK, PH.D.*, Thomas Hunter Professor in the Social Sciences, Hunter College and the Graduate Center, City University of New York; former President of the American Psychological Association (APA); former Chair, Committee on Women in Psychology, APA; incoming member, Committee on Gay Concerns, APA; former President, Division of the Psychology of Women, APA; former President, New York State Psychological Association; Board of Trustees, Association for the Advancement of Psychology. Executive Committee, National Coalition for Women's Mental Health.

NINA S. FELDMAN, PH.D., Acting Administrative Officer for Public Affairs, American Psychological Association; Adjunct Professor, Department of Psychology, University of Maryland, College Park; Member, Association of Women in Psychology; Member, Division of the Psychology of Women, American Psychological Association.

IRENE HANSON FRIEZE, PH.D., Associate Professor of Psychology, Business and Women's Studies, University of Pittsburgh, Pittsburgh, Pennsylvania; former President, Division of the Psychology of Women (Division 35), American Psychological Association (APA); former Co-chair, Division 35 Task Force on Guidelines for Nonsexist Research in Psychology; Member, APA Task Force on Victims of Crime and Violence.

JACQUELYN HALL GENTRY, PH.D., Chief, Mental Health Education Branch, National Institute of Mental Health (NIMH), Rockville, Maryland; Member, Public Health Service Task Force of Women's Health Issues; Chair, NIMH Women's Advisory Group; member, Committee on Women in Psychology, American Psychological Association; President, National Committee for Mental Health Education.

SUSAN GORE, PH.D., National Coordinator for the Association for Women in Psychology; former Executive Director and Founding Member, National Women's Studies Association; Advocacy Networks Chair, San Francisco Association of American University Women; Resource person in mental health, United Nations Decade for Psychology World Conference Planning Consultation, Vienna, Austria.

JEAN A. HAMILTON, PH.D., Director, Institute for Research on Women's Health; Private practice, Washington, D.C.; former Head, Biology of Depression Research Unit, National Institute of Mental Health, Rockville, Maryland; Research Associate and Assistant Professor, University of Chicago and Michael Reese Medical Center; Co-chair, Women's Committee, Washington Psychiatric Society; Women's Council Representative, ADAMHA.

DOROTHY HARRIS, M.S.W., Consultant to Department of Human Services, Washington, D.C.; President-Elect, National Association of Social Workers (NASW); National Coordinator of the Sixth National Conference on Child Abuse and Neglect; Member, Commission on Accreditation, Council on Social Work Education; Board of Directors, Maryland Chapter, NASW.

MARGARET HASTINGS, PH.D.*, Executive Director, Commission on Mental Health and Developmental Disabilities, State of Illinois; Government Policy and Professional Advisory Committees of National Mental Health Association; National Health Policy Committee of the American Health Planning Association; Member and former Chair of the Illinois Title XX Council; Executive Committee, National Coalition for Women's Mental Health.

NANCY A. HUMPHREYS, D.S.W.*, Director, School of Social Work, Michigan State University; past National President, National Association of Social Workers; President's Advisory Committee on Women, Carter Administration; Advisory Committee on (Legal) Professional Ethics, Supreme Court of the State of New Jersey; Commissioner, Los Angeles County Commission on Children's Institutions; Supporting Member, New Jersey Association of Hispanic Human Services Professionals; Board member, National Conference on Social Welfare.

MARY JANSEN, PH.D.*, Dean for Professional Affairs, California School of Professional Psychology; Member, Council of Representatives, American Psychological Association (APA); Chair, Committee on Women, Division of Health Psychology, APA; Chair, Continuing Education Committee, World Federation for Mental Health; Member, Subcommittee on Disability, National Mental Health Association; Editor, Rehabilitation Psychology; Executive Committee, National Coalition for Women's Mental Health.

RUTH CARLSEN KAHN, M.S.N., Chief, Nursing Education, Clinical Center Nursing Department, National Institutes of Health, Bethesda, Maryland.

LINDA SILVERMAN KING, M.S.W., L.C.S.W. Private practice in psychotherapy, Washington, D.C. and Maryland; Consultant and trainer to National Institute of Justice, Departments of Defense and Health and Human Services; former staff member, Center for Women Policy Studies, Washington, D.C.; Steering Committee Member, Women and Health Roundtable, Federation of Organizations for Professional Women.

DIANE K. KJERVIK, M.S., R.N., J.D., Director of Governmental
Relations, American Association of Colleges of Nursing, Washington, D.C.;
Associate Professor, University of Minnesota School of Nursing, Minneapolis;
Adjunct Professor, Women's Studies Program, University of Minnesota;
Commissioner, Commission on Economic and General Welfare, Minnesota
Nurses' Association.

JOYCE KOBAYASHI, M.D., Director, Psychiatric Consultation Service,
Denver General Hospital; former American Psychiatric Association/NIMH
Fellow; Member, Committee on Asian Americans in Psychiatry; Assistant
Professor of Psychiatry, University of Colorado School of Medicine.

NANCY LANE-PALES, PH.D., Administrative Officer, Professional
Services Review, American Psychological Association; Senior Program
Analyst, Dixon Implementation Office, Office of the Superintendent, St.
Elizabeth's Hospital, Washington, DC; Clinical Psychologist, Pastoral
Counseling and Consultation Centers of Greater Washington, Washington, DC.

BARBARA N. LOGAN, PH.D., Associate Professor, Psychiatric Mental
Health Nursing, University of Illinois at Chicago; former Co-Project Director,
Urban Women's Health Center, Chicago; organizer and convenor, Ethnicity and
Health Research Interest Group; Member, Illinois Nurses' Association
Commission on Research; American Nurses' Association Ethnic/Racial
Minority Fellowship Program; Legislative Intern on health issues, U.S. House
of Representatives.

ANGELA BARRON MCBRIDE, M.S.N., PH.D., Professor, Department of
Psychiatric/Mental Health Nursing, Indiana University School of Nursing;
Member, National Women's Health Network; First Vice-President, Sigma
Theta Tau (National Nursing Honor Society); Past Member, Task Force on
Public Relations, American Academy of Nursing; Past Co-convenor, Women's
Health Research Group, Midwest Nursing Research Society; Member, Social
Policy Committee, Society for Research in Child Development.

JOAN P. MEDWAY, M.ED., M.S.W., Director of Social Services,
Psychiatric Institute of Montgomery County, Maryland; Private practice and
Consultant to industry; former Chairperson of Advisory Council, Prince
George's County Family Service Aftercare, Maryland; Member, Board of Mid
Atlantic American Group Psychotherapy Association.

DOROTHY M. MILLER, M.S.W., Director, Mount Vernon Outpatient Unit,
Mount Vernon Center for Community Mental Health, Alexandria, Virginia;
Private practice; former Supervisor of social work unit, Maternal and Infant
Care Project, Department of Human Resources, Washington, D.C.; Member,
Minority Concerns Committee, Mental Health Association of Northern
Virginia; Member, Virginia State Chapter Board, National Association of Social
Workers.

MILDRED MITCHELL-BATEMAN, M.D., Professor of Psychiatry, Marshall University School of Medicine, Huntington, West Virginia; Staff Psychiatrist, Huntington VA Medical Center; Member, President's Commission on Mental Health; Chairperson, Committee on Interprofessional Affairs, American Psychiatric Association (APA); past Vice President, APA.

CAROL MOWBRAY, PH.D.*, Director, Innovations Division, Michigan Department of Mental Health (DMH); Vice-Chair, Executive Committee, State Mental Health Program Directors; Chair, Women's Issues Task Force, DMH; Committee on Women, Division of Psychologists in Public Service, American Psychological Association; Planning Committee, Michigan Mental Health Association.

CAROL NADELSON, M.D., Professor of Psychiatry, Tufts University School of Medicine, Boston, Massachusetts; President-Elect, American Psychiatric Association; Member, Executive Committee, Women's Resource Center, Department of Psychiatry, New England Medical Center; former Radcliffe Research Scholar; former President, Massachusetts Psychiatric Association; former President, Association for Academic Psychiatry; former Vice-President, Society for Sex Therapy and Research; Board of Overseers, Stone Center, Wellesley College; Board of Directors, American Psychiatric Press, Inc.

DELORES PARRON, PH.D., Associate Director for Special Populations, National Institute of Mental Health, Rockville, Maryland; former Staff Specialist to the Panel on Special Populations, President's Commission on Mental Health, Washington, D.C.; Board of Directors, Associated Catholic Charities of the Archdiocese of Washington; Member, Board of Directors, The Christ Child Institute; former member, Board of Directors, Bureau of Rehabilitation, Washington, D.C.

CAROLYN R. PAYTON, ED.D.*, Dean of Counseling and Career Development, Howard University; former Chair of the Committee on Women in Psychology, American Psychological Association (APA); former member, APA Task Force on Sex Bias and Sex-Role Stereotyping in Psychotherapeutic Practice; Member, Board of Psychologist Examiners, District of Columbia; Member, Commission on the Homeless, District of Columbia; winner of APA's Distinguished Service Award; National Coalition for Women's Mental Health.

NANCY REAME, R.N., PH.D., Associate Professor of Parent-Child Nursing, School of Nursing, University of Michigan, Ann Arbor, Michigan; Fellow, American Academy of Nursing; Editorial Board, Health Care for Women International; Board of Directors, Michigan Society for Medical Research.

PATRICIA PERRI RIEKER, PH.D., Assistant Professor, Department of Social Medicine and Health Policy, Harvard Medical School, Boston, Massachusetts; Director, Community Research and Programs, Cancer Control Division, Dana-Farber Cancer Institute, Boston.

NANCY FELIPE RUSSO, PH.D.*, Director of Women's Studies and Professor of Psychology, Arizona State University; first Administrative Officer, Women's Programs Office, American Psychological Association, Washington, D.C.; Project Director, National Women's Mental Health Agenda Conference; former President, Federation of Organizations for Professional Women; Chair, Mental Health Advisory Committee, Women and Health Roundtable and former Member of the Steering Committee; Member, Subpanel on the Mental Health of Women, President's Commission on Mental Health; Member, Long-Term Research Committee, Women's Research and Education Institute of the Congresswomen's Caucus; Chair, National Coalition for Women's Mental Health.

CAITLIN RYAN, M.S.W., Executive Director, Acquired Immune Deficiency Syndrome (AIDS) Service Agency, Atlanta, Georgia; National Task Force on Lesbian and Gay Issues, National Association of Social Workers; Project Coordinator, National Lesbian Health Care Survey/National Gay Health Education Foundation (NGHEF); President-Elect, NGHEF, New York and Washington, D.C.; Steering Committee, Federation of AIDS-related Organizations; Member, Commission on Gay/Lesbian Issues in Social Work Education, Council on Social Work Education.

STANLEY F. SCHNEIDER, PH.D., Special Assistant to the Director, Division of Human Resources, National Institute of Mental Health (NIMH), Rockville, Maryland; former Chief, Psychology Education Branch, NIMH.

NANCY SHARP, M.S.N., Associate Director for Practice and Legislation, Nurses Association of the American College of Obstetricians and Gynecologists, Washington, D.C.; former Board Member, Montgomery County Health Systems Agency, Maryland; Steering Committee, Women and Health Roundtable; President, District V, Maryland Nurses Association; Past-President, American Association of Nephrology Nurses and Technicians.

EVA STEWART, M.S.W., Professor, Howard University School of Social Work, Washington, D.C.; President, Metro Chapter - National Association of Social Workers; Member, D.C. Commission for Women; Member, Black Women's Agenda.

BONNIE STRICKLAND, PH.D.*, Professor of Psychology and Associate to the Chancellor, University of Massachusetts; former Chair, Board of Professional Affairs, American Psychological Association; former Chair, Council of Graduate Departments of Psychology; President, Division of Clinical Psychology, APA; Member, National Advisory Council on Mental Health; Member, Council of Representatives, APA, President-elect, APA.

SUSAN W. TALBOTT, R.N., M.B.A., Principal, Nurse Management Institute; President, New York Counties Registered Nurses Association; Trustee, New York State Nurses for Political Action; Member, Council on Legislation, New York State Nurses Association; Chair, Committee on Professional Education, Governor's Commission on Domestic Violence; Co-author, <u>Political Action: A Handbook for Nurses</u>; Trustee, New York State Nurses for Political Action.

NANCY E. TAYLOR, B.S., Professional Staff Member to Senator Orrin Hatch, Chairman, Committee on Labor and Human Resources for alcohol, drug abuse and mental health issues; Candidate for the J.D. Degree, Catholic University of America.

REIKO HOMMA TRUE, M.S.W., PH.D.*, Area Deputy Director for Adult Services, San Francisco City and County Community Mental Health Services; Vice Chair, Committee on Women in Psychology, American Psychological Association (APA); Chair, Task Force on Asian Women, Division of the Psychology of Women, APA; Board of Directors, Asian American Psychological Association; Member, Quality Assurance and Minority Services Committees, California State Psychological Association; Treasurer, Asian Women United.

DIANA M. ZUCKERMAN, PH.D., National Policy Associate, National Policy Studies, American Psychological Association (APA), Washington, D.C.; Congressional Science Fellow, APA; former Director, Seven College Study, Radcliffe College, Harvard University, Cambridge, Massachusetts; former Postdoctoral Fellow in Psychosocial Epidemiology, Yale University School of Medicine, New Haven, Connecticut.